To Leeann &
With Love
From Dad & Mum xxx
Christmas 2002 at Mettven
New Zealand

GLORIOUS OLD ROSES

VIKING

GLORIOUS OLD ROSES

TREVOR GRIFFITHS

VIKING

AN IMPRINT OF PENGUIN BOOKS

VIKING An imprint of Penguin Books

Penguin Books (NZ) Ltd, cnr Rosedale
and Airborne Roads, Albany,
Auckland 1310, New Zealand
Penguin Books Ltd, 27 Wrights Lane,
London W8 5TZ, England
Penguin Putnam Inc, 375 Hudson Street,
New York, NY 10014, United States
Penguin Books Australia Ltd,
487 Maroondah Highway, Ringwood,
Australia 3134
Penguin Books Canada Ltd, 10 Alcorn
Avenue, Toronto, Ontario,
Canada M4V 3B2
Penguin Books (South Africa) Pty Ltd,
5 Watkins Street, Denver Ext 4, 2094,
South Africa
Penguin Books India (P) Ltd,
11, Community Centre, Panchsheel Park,
New Delhi 110 017, India

Penguin Books Ltd, Registered Offices:
Harmondsworth, Middlesex, England

First published in 2000
10 9 8 7 6 5 4 3 2 1

Designed and typeset by
Athena Sommerfeld
Printed by Bookbuilders, Hong Kong
ISBN 0 670 89431 1

Acknowledgement is gratefully given to
David Austin Roses of Wolverhampton,
England, for the use of his colour plates
for this volume.

Thanks also to Colin Hutchinson for the
use of photographs on pp. 82, 147 and
to Random House Australia for the use
of photographs on pp. 42, 60, 76, 86, 161,
173, 185.

The publishers would like to thank Gill
Ward of Victorian Gilt, Auckland, and
Sheridan Keith of Antiques and Angels,
Auckland, for the use of antique linen
and paper.

Illustrations:
P 1. Eglantyne
P 2. Evelyn
P 3. William Morris
P 6. Saint Swithun
P 8. Teasing Georgia
P 20. Louise Odier

CONTENTS

FOREWORD

Since the decline of the old roses towards the end of the
nineteenth century, the rose world has been blessed with a
number of pioneering nurserymen in various countries who
have made it their business to reintroduce old roses to the
gardening public: first of all, A. E. Bunyard, and later, Graham
Thomas in Britain, Neilson in Denmark, Francis E. Lester, and
Wylie, to name but a few.

Trevor Griffiths, the well-known New Zealand
nurseryman, must be rated among these pioneers.
His work in putting together his large collection
of old roses has done much to make them popular in his country and beyond. Trevor has had the
good fortune to live in a country of keen gardeners and rosarians, without whom his work would
not have been possible, or necessary.

It may seem strange that such beautiful roses as
the Gallicas, the Damask roses, the Albas, and so
on, should ever have fallen from popularity. However, the Hybrid Teas, and later the Floribundas,
had the advantage that they were very free-
flowering over a long period and had a very wide
colour range. It was not long before gardeners
began to appreciate that these roses lacked some
of the charm, the elegance of growth and the rich

fragrance of the old roses, which are now widely
grown throughout the gardening world. Trevor
Griffiths can take a large measure of credit for the
revival of the old roses in New Zealand – and not
a little credit for their present popularity throughout the world.

It has been my privilege to know Trevor Griffiths
for many years now and I regard him as a friend.
Anyone who has walked with him, as I have,
around his collection of roses, cannot fail to have
been impressed by his knowledge and love of
roses. He has given us a number of very interesting books on old roses, all of them illustrated with
his own excellent photographs. These have always
been well received and I am quite sure that this
latest will be greeted with equal enthusiasm.

David Austin

IT WAS NOT
IN THE WINTER
OUR LOVING LOT WAS CAST!
IT WAS THE TIME OF ROSES,
WE PLUCKED THEM
AS WE PASSED!

THOMAS HOOD, 1799–1845

INTRODUCTION

The object of this book is to bring before the gardeners of the world at large the beauty of glorious old roses. It is now many years since my pen was first placed on paper to record my life's work with roses, and although many things have happened to lead me away from my favourite subject, my resolve for the family at large has never been shaken. There has been an awakening towards old roses, which I believe will result in them staying in our homes and our hearts for more than the foreseeable future. Over the last fifty years or so, two changes have affected the popularity of old roses. The first great change has come from the tens of thousands of old rose enthusiasts in every country who have come to admire the attributes of old roses, which include durability, health, toughness, beauty, fragrance, disease resistance, medicinal uses and longevity. The second great change is twofold and still in the process of development. This is the changed attitude towards the look of roses in the future, and the acceptance by hybridisers in every country that there is life beyond Hybrid Teas.

Many years have passed since I had the temerity to predict that the Hybrid Tea class of roses was being superseded. This was based on the assumption that of the many families of roses that have come and gone – some of short duration and some of long duration – over the space of 200 years or more, it was inevitable that the insatiable desire of people wanting something different would prevail. The change in hybridisers' attitudes helped as well. The capacity for change has always been inherent in the genus *Rosa*, but few were prepared to chance their arm, as it were, and set up a programme to achieve this. The coming of roses such as 'Nozomi', 'Immensee', and many others brought changes that could not be believed. Perhaps change did not seem achievable when hybridists all used varieties that were similar, but when they went backwards in time and realised the wealth of hidden genes in the old families, change was bound to come.

Some of the older established rose breeders had been working along these lines for many years when it suited them but it was not until David Austin of England appeared on the scene that real progress was made. It is possible that during the early parts of his breeding programme even he did not realise the importance of his work, but looking back over more than thirty years the changes made are obvious for all to see. The depth of the gene pool he has opened up has hardly been touched and his foresight and work will be cemented into the history of roses so that future generations will always be reminded of his inspirational work. He had a vision that, fortunately for rose growers, he was able to pursue. He has declared many times that early on in his work he was driven by the desire to try to make the old roses such as the Gallicas, Damasks, and Albas flower again in one season, and anyone who has read his books will know that he has achieved this admirably. Throughout history there have been

men and women of vision and although many of them have passed from view and never reached their goals, others have been fortunate in doing so. David Austin has been, and still is, a rose grower and breeder who has had those elusive factors of time, opportunity, and finance come together to allow him to spend many years pursuing his dream. Added to this, of course, he was a comparatively young man when he first delved into the genes of the genus *Rosa*.

In my eyes, David Austin has been the right man at the right time. At a period of life when others of lesser mettle would have given away their lifetime trade or profession for a pipe and the bowling green, David still has the inner urge to go on creating something even more beautiful, durable, colourful and fragrant than he has before. The glorious old roses he has created can at times leave you breathless, surprised, contented, and even tearful. It is inevitable that his work will remain a glimmering beacon, a monument to the tenacity of man, a tribute to an ex-farmer who could think beyond the square.

The David Austin roses have spread across the world, and thousands admire them. Some criticise them, but too often this is born from ignorance or jealousy. It is true that some varieties do not do well in some conditions but, in the main, because they derive partially from the old families, they have a toughness and a will to survive that the so-called modern roses can only dream about. The early produced varieties closely resembled some of the old Gallicas, Damasks and others, but as the development programme progressed, unusual colours and forms appeared – you could say by-products of the intended direction. Some of the most intense deep yellows and golds have also come forward. One has to wonder what some of the great French rose breeders such as Pernet-Ducher, Barbier or Vibert would say if they could see these colours today.

After a lifetime of growing, collecting, and producing roses, there is no doubt in my mind that David Austin has done more to change roses as we know them than any other rose grower and breeder. We, the customers of the world, have been privileged to be present while this was happening, and more than privileged to be able to grow many of them.

IT WAS ROSES, ROSES, ALL THE WAY
ROBERT BROWNING, 1812–1889

The term 'old rose' is often misused and misunderstood. To appreciate the subject and the family as a whole we must accept that we are dealing with roses from the beginning of time. Whilst roses collected by cutting or root from the Civil War cemeteries of the United States of America, the goldfields of New Zealand or Australia, or the historical homes and castles of Europe are old, they come from a time zone that is limited to not much more than 100 years. This leaves many thousands of years unaccounted for and it is my intention to convert the reader to an appreciation of the wider world of old roses. It was not by accident that my first book was named *My World of Old Roses*, and it is not unintentional that this volume is called *Glorious Old Roses*.

To discuss this matter fully one has to realise that the term 'old' is used in its widest sense. To call these beautiful members historical or heritage roses is simply not good enough. Both titles are partially correct but are certainly not comprehensive enough in their definition. One might successfully ask which history or rather whose history makes them historical and in like fashion whose heritage we are talking about. Both terms could be appropriate for small geographical areas but are definitely not adequate when looking at the wider picture of thirty to forty million years of the Earth's evolution or the distribution areas of the genus *Rosa* across the Earth's surface, either naturally or by humans.

Apart from the accepted fact that roses were in the northern hemisphere landscape when humans in their several forms arrived on earth, there is little doubt that with the inevitable movement of those early peoples, they transported not only the members of their extended families from site to site, but also their animals and all the plants that would provide them with food and healing potions and medicines. It is also more than a little possible that roses were translocated by early civilisations for other reasons. They were a ready-made source of firewood for the quick starting of campfires and more often than not became symbols of people's beliefs and even superstitions. Much folklore relates to this. It would not have been long before the early races realised the wealth of benefits available from the plant world surrounding them, and nor would they have been slow to realise that many of those sources of benefit could be dried or preserved in some way to provide assistance during the long winters experienced in the northern parts of the northern hemisphere.

As the centuries and ages went by and *Homo sapiens* developed, if that is the correct term, so the demands of those peoples increased. It would be fair to say that for whatever reason man moved over the Earth's surface, be it warlike, peaceful or even just plain curiosity, roses went with him. Their fragrances, their medicinal properties, their beauty, their ability to survive, and their other properties were enough to ensure their popularity. Even from these early times old roses were revered and worshipped.

OH, NO MAN KNOWS
THROUGH WHAT WILD CENTURIES
ROVES BACK THE ROSE
WALTER DE LA MARE, 1873–1956

The number one problem with old roses – in fact any rose – will always be correct identification. Some collectors or students of the genus do a lot of research on a particular rose or group of roses and, because their particular specimen fits rather neatly into a certain time zone and answers to a description in a book or catalogue, they assume that they have found its correct name. Identification consists not only of the examination of the flower in all its stages, but also, probably more importantly, careful inspection of the leaves, the prickles, the wood, and any other distinguishing features that could show it to be different from another. The one factor that seems to be given little credence by rose researchers and rose rustlers alike is the inbuilt ability of the members of the genus to survive and, because of this amazing survival rate, today's students can be quite easily deceived.

Aside from the ongoing problem of identification, the next most difficult task is to work one's way through the massive time zone from the moment roses first appeared in the Earth's landscape to the period of time when they were first described in early publications. After early mention of the genus by various historians, there were genuine attempts to describe in detail certain varieties. Today's enthusiasts are confounded by the fact that these early writers did not have access to computers or cameras. Nevertheless attempts were made to record these early discoveries and it is the interpretation of these descriptions that causes confusion today. One has enough difficulty trying to grasp a description of a rose from a person standing beside you, let alone struggling with one from

several hundred years ago, or even from some years ago.

Many roses have been deliberately planted in many different places, and at certain times during their lifetime, which eventually comes to an end, there can be expressed within the plant the wish to recreate itself before it is summoned from this probationary scene. The result can often be a seedling surviving quite close to where its parent may have been able to grow happily for a hundred years. This then creates a problem. We now have a rose similar in many respects to the parent but different in other ways. A piece of this new creation can be mistaken for the original, and propagated and distributed, thus compounding the already complex identification problem. After a lifetime of working with roses, and everything that means, one becomes very suspicious when a strange rose is presented for identification.

Another facet of this very involved and complex subject is the pronunciation of names. Taking the family as a whole, many names appear to be difficult for English-speaking admirers to pronounce, and botanical names of species can also be a problem. However, as a grower of roses for fifty years or more, my experience was always that customers made themselves understood even when the names were awkward for them.

Some years ago I had the privilege of visiting Castle Howard in Yorkshire, England, and was invited by Jim Russell, the curator, to stay for dinner. Imagine my excitement and surprise when the other dinner guest was Graham Thomas. During the evening the conversation ranged far and wide about things horticultural when we reached an inevitable discussion on David Austin roses. The subject was given a good hearing, and when I mentioned that great English plantswoman Gertrude Jekyll, Graham intervened with, 'Tut tut, Trevor, Jekyll rhymes with treacle.'

Names are very important to plants and naturally they need them for identification, but when a rose is introduced under a certain name, no one has the right to change it. The raiser must have an inviolable right to name as he pleases. Quite a few years ago I was fortunate enough to locate two hybrid *Banksiae* roses. After years of searching they were found in Denmark and the usual arrangements were made for me to import them into New Zealand. The roses were 'Hybrid Di Castello' and 'Purezza', both raised by Mansuino of Italy. Over the years they were available to the public they never gained the popularity they should have, perhaps through my neglect, but 'Purezza' did find its way into the hands of an unscrupulous grower who renamed it 'The Pearl' and propagated tens of thousands for quick sales.

Fortunately, now that the Plant Protection Act has come into being, a rose is adequately protected from all forms of free market forces, but those that do not enjoy this protection are open to the pirates within the trade who give not one jot for ethics.

The protection process, which was the brainchild of Sam McGredy, was introduced into New Zealand some twenty years ago. When new varieties are created, they are passed on to an agent for distribution. In our particular case, the start of the process is an application for a permit from the Ministry of Agriculture, in which is specified the country of origin of the rose material, the number required, and the names of those we wish to import. The permit is issued for a specified period only, and the material concerned must be in quarantine for two growing seasons. During this time the plants are inspected by the Ministry's officers and, if nothing detrimental to the health of the plants is found, they are released and we are then able to propagate them to build up the numbers for distribution across New Zealand. This process takes four years from the time of application for the permit.

The next step is an application to enter the varieties into the Plant Protection Rights process. These entries must be placed with the Plant Varieties Rights Office in Lincoln College before the 30th

16

of March each year. The next part of the process is to send six plants of each variety entered for the Plant Varieties Rights (P.V.R.) system to the test garden in Palmerston North by mid-July each year for examination by a panel of experts. If nothing untoward happens, a certificate is issued stating that the variety is now protected under the Plant Protection Act for the next twenty-three years. Many of the finer points of this system have not been mentioned, but two deserve to be detailed.

When the rose material arrives from overseas it comes in the form of budwood – that is, two or three pieces of wood taken from the plant just below a spent flower. This wood, which is about the size of a lead pencil, will have about five or six growth buds on it and these are removed and inserted into a rootstock, one to each stock, and hopefully, if the wood arrived in fresh condition, most of them will grow. The other point that requires elaboration is the cost of the whole process. For the permit, packing, airfreight, quarantine site and fees, P.V.R. application, entry into the test garden, issue of the certificate and renewal for one year, at least $1500 is required, and this sum does not allow for the man hours and materials that are required.

The end result is that the raiser now has his rose protected from piracy in all of the countries that subscribe to the system, meaning that a royalty is collected on the raiser's behalf for every rose grown. The Rose Introducers of New Zealand (R.I.N.Z.) is the collecting body for royalties, and their officers visit all the growers and count the protected varieties budded. When the count is complete, each grower pays the R.I.N.Z., who then assembles the funds by a due date each year. Each agent receives the allocation for his particular agencies, who are then recompensed for that year's roses grown under the protection system. It is a very fair system, which quite literally protects the raiser from piracy of his rights. If a rose has been protected, it will bear the term 'Protected Variety' on its nursery label.

Several years ago we had reason to suspect that a certain grower was obtaining new rose varieties from England by means of an illegal process. The rose plants were bought in garden centres as they were released onto the English market, packed for safe transport to New Zealand (without the necessary permits) and sent to several people who were either colleagues or relatives of the person behind the illegal scheme. On arrival in New Zealand the plants were intercepted by Ministry officials who, after much investigation, decided not to prosecute the offender. Of course this action was not acceptable and leaves us wondering about the usefulness of the Ministry.

There is sometimes confusion about the use of rootstocks for the increase of roses. A long time ago it was discovered that many of nature's creations actually developed better when growing on another, often related, root system. Different countries not only use different rootstocks but also use various methods of increasing them. In New Zealand we use *R. multiflora* stocks grown from cuttings while United States growers mainly use a stockknown as 'Dr Huey', and most European and United Kingdom growers use a group of stocks all grown from seed. These are *R. laxa, R. inermis, R. canina, R. rugosa, R. eglanteria*, and sometimes *R. multiflora*.

It is well known that the main methods of reproduction in plants are by growing from seed or increasing by cuttings. Both methods have inherent advantages and disadvantages, which become very apparent as you explore the exciting world of creating new plants. Sometimes I believe that Mother Nature watches over bumbling attempts with a jaundiced eye and a smile on her face.

Rose plants grown from seedling stocks are generally free from disease while those on stock grown from cuttings are prone to several diseases. Herein lies the problem. Those millions of roses grown in Europe on seedling stocks of whatever name have a great start in life because their base is virus free,

but simply because they are increased in this way does not prevent them from sending up suckers from the base for the rest of their lives. You may ask why this should be, and rightly so. Perhaps it can be explained in this way. Nurserymen and plant growers everywhere know that when a plant of any type begins to show signs of not wanting to grow and develop, the best possible treatment is to cut it back quite severely. The reasoning behind this action is that all plants have above the root system, although they are not visible, what are called adventitious shoots, which mostly remain dormant until they receive a check or knock-back of some kind. The cutting-back process will work nine times out of ten. Over the years many roses have been returned to us showing no signs of life whatsoever. Cut back to about 2.5cm from the union, potted and looked after, they mostly would grow, and great was my delight when several months later I could show the customer the very plant that had been proclaimed dead, happily in flower.

Thus rose plants grafted onto a seed-grown rootstock can, by virtue of their adventitious shoots, sucker merrily for the rest of their days. Some years ago, in a country that can remain nameless, a field of nearly a million roses had more suckers present than shoots from real roses, and one must ask how these beautiful varieties were presented to the public at selling time.

The growing of cutting-grown rootstocks must also be discussed to present a balanced picture to the reader. Obviously large beds of material must be maintained and replaced from time to time to enable a grower to take enough cuttings to satisfy the numbers required for a particular season. All the eyes except the top two or three are removed from the cuttings with a sharp knife. They can then either be placed in sand for a couple of months to callous, or planted directly into the field provided moisture is available to keep them alive until they have rooted. Both seedling and cutting stock must be kept growing until they are budded or grafted, which of course requires a free flow of sap to be successful.

Here lie the major differences between the two processes. The former is virus free and produces medium-sized bushes that have the ability to sucker, while the latter can contain viruses that are passed on to the plant, have larger growth systems, and do not sucker. Some of each system can produce the best results, that is, stock beds grown from seed and made into cuttings with continual renewal of the stock beds from seed. One final comment is required, and that is that rose plants of any kind grown from seed have always been known to be disease and virus free.

There is a movement in New Zealand to enforce a virus-free rootstock growing programme on rose growers, and although this system has high ideals and good intentions, the programme is very costly and difficult to enforce. It may be that the buying public do not care about it, and those who persist in producing cutting-grown rose plants for sale will never achieve that status.

PHYSICIANS OF THE UTMOST FAME
WERE CALLED AT ONCE, BUT WHEN THEY CAME
THEY ANSWERED, AS THEY TOOK THEIR FEES
'THERE IS NO CURE FOR THIS DISEASE'
HILAIRE BELLOC, 1870–1953

THE ROSES

I WOULD RATHER HAVE ONE LITTLE ROSE,
FROM THE GARDEN OF A FRIEND,
THAN TO HAVE THE CHOICEST FLOWERS
WHEN MY STAY ON EARTH MUST END

ANON

To arrange the rose varieties alphabetically on this occasion seems to be the best decision, but of course with all choices there are bound to be some disadvantages. Each rose discussed has a picture and a description covering all aspects of its particular history and its requirements. As regards the term 'old rose', this will once again be used in the broadest possible sense, that is, it will be the form of the flower and not its date of introduction that will see it included in this volume. The reader would be wise to remember that there are thousands of old roses still available worldwide, and it is my intention to write about only several hundred, chosen on their popularity and availability.

ABRAHAM DARBY

Raised by David Austin, United Kingdom
Parentage 'Yellow Cushion' x 'Aloha'
Introduced 1985
Type English Rose
Size 2m x 2m and more

It is appropriate that the first rose to be listed and discussed in this book should be one of many talents. It is one of David Austin's earliest introductions and, strange as it may seem, both of its parents are comparatively modern. Nevertheless it has all the attributes of an old type rose. It adopts a lovely rounded shrub-like appearance, has the most attractive glossy green foliage, with large quite double blooms, cupped and extremely fragrant. The colour is coppery-apricot at first, turning to peachy-pink with age. In the right situation it can be grown as a climber and is not at all difficult to grow on a trellis or archway. In fact when grown as a climber the large heavy flowers can better be seen, especially after rain.

←— *previous page*

ACICULARIS

Arctic Rose, North America
Parentage Natural distribution
Distribution 1805
Type Species
Size 1m and upright

Here is a species that is not very well known although its distribution area and that of its close relations spreads over vast areas of Finland, Canada, Japan, North East Asia and Northern Europe. Its toughness is apparent from the areas in which it grows and it has been described to me by people who have visited the Tundra in Alaska. The flowers are an attractive rose to cerise pink, single and semi-double, sometimes up to 50mm wide, with yellow stamens. The foliage is light green and rather dull while the stems are covered with many small prickles. The fragrant blooms are followed by bristly pear-shaped fruits, which are bright red and can be up to 20mm long. In warmer situations late flowers are quite prevalent.

ADÉLAÏDE D'ORLÉANS

Raised by *Jacques*
Parentage *Unknown*
Introduced *1826*
Type *Rambler*
Size *Up to 5m*

At one time in our history there were only once-flowering ramblers available to garden enthusiasts, and this was one of the very best. It obviously has what is known as Ayrshire blood in it and no doubt this is where its beauty and durability comes from. Its floral display is quite outstanding and needs to be looked up to in order to fully appreciate the beauty of the blooms. They develop from clusters of reddish rounded buds and burst out into quite double cupped flowers of blush pink fading to white and are quite fragrant. When in flower this rose has been likened to a flowering cherry at its best.

AGNES

Raised by *Saunders*
Parentage *R. rugosa x R. persiana*
Introduced *1922*
Type *Hybrid Rugosa*
Size *2m x 1.5m*

Rugosa roses, natives of Japan and Korea, took a long time to gain a measure of popularity, and this variety, although it is a hybrid, is one member of the larger family that has immeasurably helped the situation. Whether by accident or design the creation of this beautiful variety brought into the family a colour that was not previously present. Its flowers are medium to large and loosely double, and when the summer display is at its best it surely is a sight to behold. They are coppery-yellow and have a delicious scent with intermittent blooms later. This is one of the few roses that are truly disease free.

AÏCHA

Raised by *Valdemar Petersen*
Parentage *Unknown*
Introduced *1966*
Type *Shrub-climber*
Size *2m x 1m*

During my association with Valdemar Petersen of Löve, Denmark, I was very fortunate to receive from his old roses many that were unobtainable elsewhere and, more importantly, I was safe in the knowledge that they were accurately named. Every season when my budwood arrived there were always added to the consignment one or two I had not asked for, which were in fact Valdemar's own varieties. This is how I came to get 'Aïcha', an upright plant with prickly stems and healthy foliage. The blooms are large (12cm or more), golden yellow at first, fading lighter with five or more large petals and a concentration of large stamens in the middle. It is a useful plant for the back of the border or shrubbery.

1
ALAIN BLANCHARD

Raised by *Vibert*
Parentage *Unknown*
Introduced *1839*
Type *Gallica*
Size *1m x 1m*

Many of the early Gallicas were raised by simply collecting seed vessels from established plants and sowing them in their thousands in rows in the fields, from which suitable selections were made. No doubt this variety arrived in this way. Even after all this time it is one of the unusual members of the family in that the purplish-crimson double blooms become mottled or spotted as they develop. They are fragrant, large, and have golden stamens.

2
ALBA

Raised by *Origin unknown*
Parentage *A white form*
of R. rugosa
Introduced *Prior to 1799*
Type *Hybrid Rugosa*
Size *2m x 2m*

As already stated, this family is indigenous to Korea and Japan. The true members of the genus usually have large flowers followed by considerable amounts of large fruit. Coming from some of the northern-most countries they are perfectly hardy under almost any conditions and they have the added attribute of flowering and fruiting almost continuously. This particular variety has large, single Persil-white flowers with yellow stamens of unquestionable beauty. They are fragrant and followed by a crop of large shiny orange fruit and are very attractive in the autumn before the hungry birds start on them.

3
ALBÉRIC BARBIER

Raised by *Barbier*
Parentage *R.wichuraiana*
x 'Shirley Hibberd'
Introduced *1900*
Type *Rambler*
Size *6m x 6m*

For many years this rose was accepted as the definitive rambling rose. It seems to have been popular in many countries. Its ease of establishment under all types of conditions, its rapid growth, its healthy green foliage, its medium-sized double flowers, its fruity fragrance, its ability to grow into trees and unsightly places, its medium-sized double flowers, which are yellow in the bud opening to creamy white with a good second crop, are the attributes that have made this rose one of the most recognisable of the old ones. Much work could be done by modern hybridisers to make a new race of ramblers ever-blooming.

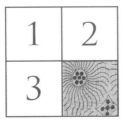

1
ALBERTINE

Raised by *Barbier*
Parentage *R. wichuraiana x 'Mrs A. R. Waddell'*
Introduced *1921*
Type *Rambler*
Size *6m x 6m*

During the European summer of 1985 it was my privilege to visit the Western countries of this vast area. As a rose grower on his first tour of these countries the roses in flower naturally took my eye, and the one that stood out among all others was 'Albertine'. Yes, it flowers but once a season but its performance is exquisite. A powerful grower, very healthy growth, a degree of toughness known in few other ramblers, and a marvellous display of bloom in mid-summer are the hallmarks of this famous rose. The flowers can be up to 15cm across, are quite double and open to bronzy salmon-pink from fat reddish-salmon buds. The floral display can extend over six to eight weeks.

| 1 | 2 | 3 |
| | 4 | 5 |

2
ALCHEMIST

Raised by *Kordes*
Parentage *'Golden Glow' x R. rubiginosa hybrid*
Introduced *1956*
Type *Shrub-climber*
Size *4m x 3m*

Mention was made in the introduction of this volume to several hybridisers who over the years have gone backwards in time with one parent in their present-day work, and this beautiful rose is the product of this thinking. The flowers are large, up to 12cm across, very double and golden-yellow at first deepening to orange in the centre. They are quartered as in the old rose manner and have quite a strong fragrance. This is one of the loveliest roses in its class and is recommended for all situations.

3
ALEXANDRE GIRAULT

Raised by *Barbier*
Parentage *R. wichuraiana x 'Papa Gontier'*
Introduced *1909*
Type *Rambler*
Size *6m x 6m*

The French rose grower and hybridist, Barbier, was responsible for the introduction of many extremely beautiful rambling roses, and this is another. When considering whether or not to grow non-recurrent roses, do not forget that they have a flowering season of at least six to eight weeks, and this period fits into the gap between the two main seasons of a repeat-flowering variety. Also, a once-a-season flowering rose has a longer period of bloom than the average rhododendron, camellia or azalea. Very fragrant medium-sized quartered blooms of reddish cerise-pink with lemon centres, together with healthy foliage, are the excellent attributes of this variety.

4
ALFRED DE DALMAS

Raised by *Laffay*
Parentage *Unknown*
Introduced *1855*
Type *Moss*
Size *1m x 1m*

A Moss rose of some importance. Its colour is blush-pink opening from fat medium-pink buds, which have a good scent. It has upright prickly growth with light green foliage. This variety has some ability to flower again later in the season. Many Moss roses flower once only but those that have mixed parentage often have a recurrent gene installed into them.

5
ALISTER STELLA GRAY

Raised by *Gray*
Parentage *Unknown*
Introduced *1894*
Type *Noisette*
Size *5m or more*

This rose introduces the Noisette family to this volume. They are an amazing and exceptional group and although not large in number have had a great effect on our appreciation of old roses in general and the creation of new varieties in particular. It is my belief that this rose has been confused with others but in spite of this it is a magnificent rose having small, very double blooms produced in profusion over a very long period. They are yolk-yellow at first with developing light orange centres fading to lighter shades, with a pleasing scent.

ALLEN CHANDLER

Raised by *Prince*
Parentage *'Hugh Dickson' x seedling*
Introduced *1923*
Type *Climber*
Size *4m x 3m*

A very useful rose that does not seem to be so popular today but nevertheless has some excellent attributes, not least its beautiful deep crimson colour, which tends to move to purplish-crimson as it ages. It has large flowers up to 10–12cm across, which are more semi-double than single, and the golden stamens sit up attractively in the middle. Lightly fragrant, it has healthy growth with dark green foliage and can produce large orange-red fruit in the autumn. Recurrent.

AMBRIDGE ROSE

Raised by *David Austin*
Parentage *'Charles Austin' x seedling*
Introduced *1990*
Type *English Rose*
Size *1m x 1m*

A rose of some quality but not a large grower, very useful for bedding purposes or for the front of a border. Its upright growth and bright green foliage are quite distinctive. The blooms, which are double and of medium size, sit up nicely on strong stems and are orange-yellow and quite fragrant.

opposite ⟶

AMÉLIA

Raised by *Vibert*
Parentage *Unknown*
Introduced *1823*
Type *Alba*
Size *1m x 1m*

Here we have a fine member of the Alba group with its grey-green foliage and inbuilt toughness and durability. This ancient family was known during the Middle Ages and generally are of upright growth, with this rose having attractive large double flowers of medium to pale pink with a strong scent.

AMERICAN PILLAR

Raised by *Van Fleet*
Parentage *(R. wichuraiana x R. setigera) x 'Red Hybrid Perpetual'*
Introduced *1902*
Type *Rambler*
Size *10m or more*

Although this old rose does not get good reports from some quarters, the fact remains that it grows in places where no other rose can survive. It has amazing vitality and durability. It can be seen near the sea where from time to time it is showered with salt water; it can be seen at altitudes where the heat of summer and the cold of winter would destroy most other roses; it can be seen in many places in between, and always it looks well with its dark green foliage and its medium-sized single flowers, mostly scarlet with a white eye. It is often found in old cemeteries and goldfield sites – its toughness is beyond reproach. It has no apparent scent and is summer-flowering only.

ANÄIS SÉGALES

Raised by *Vibert*
Parentage *Unknown*
Introduced *1837*
Type *Gallica*
Size *1.5m x 1m*

This is one of the first roses to arrive in New Zealand with the early settlers and in many places it has become naturalised. It has colours that took material manufacturers a long time to achieve. Of the large group of Gallicas now available, this variety would be one of the most sought after. The reason for this probably lies in its colour, which is deep mauvish-crimson paling to a very pretty lilac-pink with age, a very popular and contemporary set of colours for today's fashions. The shape of the blooms is considered perfect, being flat and quite double with a green eye in the centre. It is very fragrant and summer-flowering only.

ANGELINA

Raised by *Cocker*
Parentage *('Tropicana' x 'Carine') x ('Cläre Grammerstorf x 'Frühlingsmorgen')*
Introduced *1976*
Type *Shrub-climber*
Size *3m*

Another fine variety that has originated from breeding from an old rose type. The plant can make three or more metres in height and be covered in 9cm blooms of rose-pink round the edges and white in the centre, which are semi-double in habit. A superb shrub that can create a bright spot in any border. It has a lovely scent.

ANNA-MARIA DE MONTRAVEL

Raised by *Unknown*
Parentage *Unknown*
Introduced *1880*
Type *China Hybrid*
Size *1m x 1m*

The members of the China family are many and varied, and come to the Western world from many parts of that vast country. It is recognised that probably two-thirds of the world's native roses come from the South-East Asia region and it is certain that there must have been some form of rose breeding taking place, although there appear to be no records of this happening. This variety is a small-growing rounded plant with light green healthy foliage and has clusters of small, double, purest-white blooms, which put on a brave show all summer long.

ANNE BOLEYN

Raised by *David Austin*
Parentage *Unknown*
Introduced *1999*
Type *English Rose*
Size *1.5m*

A very new addition to the English Rose family, having been released for the first time at the Chelsea Flower Show in May 1999. Lightly fragrant, this rose produces large sprays of rosette-shaped warm pink blossoms with remarkable continuity. No doubt 'Anne Boleyn' will become a fine addition to the large group of pink English Roses.

ARETHUSA

Raised by *Paul*
Parentage *Unknown*
Introduced *1903*
Type *China Hybrid*
Size *1m x 1m*

As with the previous China hybrid mentioned, this beautiful rose grows to a rounded shrub of about 1m tall and wide. Its dark green glossy foliage is a lovely background for the deep apricot buds opening to lighter apricot loosely double blooms, which have a pleasant fragrance. Ideal for smaller gardens.

ARTHUR HILLIER

Raised by *Hillier*
Parentage *R. macrophylla x R. moyesii*
Introduced *1961*
Type *Shrub*
Size *3m x 3m*

Here we have a rose that is not very well known but would be a valuable addition to any large garden. The rosy-crimson single five-petalled blooms are about 8cm across with yellow stamens in the centre. As with all roses with *R. moyesii* as a parent, these blooms are followed by magnificent flagon-shaped fruit, bright orange-red, nicely backed by dark green foliage.

ARVENSIS

Raised by *Native to UK and Europe*
Parentage *Unknown*
Introduction *Ancient*
Type *Species*
Size *5m x 5m*

Mentioned by Shakespeare in his writings, this variety is known commonly as the Field Rose. There is little doubt that it has had a part to play in the parentage of many old roses. It is a prolific grower with long wiry stems produced in all directions. Single white flowers of about 5 to 7cm across have bright yellow stamens followed by small oval-shaped bright red fruit. When growing profusely in the country-side, it is not hard to see where the name 'Rose of the Field' comes from.

A SHROPSHIRE LAD

Raised by *David Austin*
Parentage *Unknown*
Introduced *1996*
Type *English Rose*
Size *1.5m x 1.5m*

A fairly recent introduction, which of course brings back memories of 'Leander', from which it is bred. Like its parent, it is tall growing and has healthy disease-free foliage, which always looks well. The lightly cupped blooms open to peachy-apricot and deep apricot in the centre. They have a delicious fragrance. A beautiful rose fit for any garden.

opposite →

ASH WEDNESDAY

Raised by *Kordes*
Parentage *R. rubiginosa hybrid*
Introduced *1955*
Type *Shrub-climber*
Size *3m x 3m*

Fittingly named, this excellent hybrid really has greyish-white blooms of medium to large size opening from silvery-grey buds. They have a pleasant scent and at times can have a pale coppery or brownish shading deep in the flower. The edge of the petals are cut or fluted, which makes the overall flower rather attractive and different.

← *opposite*

ATROPURPUREA

Raised by *Paul*
Parentage *R. rugosa x R. damascena*
Introduced *1899*
Type *Hybrid Rugosa*
Size *1m x 1m*

Over the years many Rugosas and their hybrids have been discovered in gardens from all over the world. This particular variety, although it was raised in England and rediscovered in Denmark, is very much up to the standard of the other members of the group. Often rose flowers pale towards the centre but in this case the pretty shade of carmine-crimson of the medium to large single blooms keeps its colour right into the golden stamens.

AUGUSTE GERVAIS

Raised by *Barbier*
Parentage *R. wichuraiana x 'Le Progrés'*
Introduced *1918*
Type *Rambler*
Size *6m x 6m*

Barbier, the French raiser of many roses, was responsible for this gem, and it is one of his best. The growth is very vigorous with long branches in all directions if allowed. It is an ideal covering plant. Added to this is the extreme beauty of the flowers, which can be 8–10cm across and open quite flat. The blooms have short petals and are abundantly produced against the dark glossy foliage, which always looks well. When open the flowers are coppery-salmon and lemon and are strongly scented. What more could one ask?

AUTUMNALIS

Raiser and parentage *Unknown*
Introduced *1812*
Type *Noisette*
Size *3m x 3m*

Although the parentage and origins are not known it does not prevent it from being a very interesting rose. Under sheltered conditions it could easily remain quite evergreen. There is a strong resemblance to both 'Annie Vibert' and 'Aimée Vibert', and it is possible that the three of them came from the same source. 'Autumnalis' has, as its name suggests, an abundance of flowers in the autumn, which are double and creamy-white backed by light green dense foliage.

AUTUMN DELIGHT

Raised by *Bentall*
Parentage *Unknown*
Introduced *1933*
Type *Hybrid Musk*
Size *1m x 1m*

This family could be described as the forerunners of the Floribunda class and in reality, although they are called Musks, they have precious little Musk in them. However, this variety is a very good example. It has large clusters of almost single flowers, which stand uprightly on a plant that grows to over a metre. Red stamens are prominent in the centre of the flower, which is extremely fragrant. The colour is pale buff-yellow in the bud opening to white or creamy-white. It has greenish medium-sized fruit.

AWAKENING

Marketed by *Beales*
Parentage *'New Dawn' sport*
Introduced *1992*
Type *Climber*
Size *5m x 5m*

Most rose enthusiasts would know the rose 'New Dawn' which is the parent of 'Awakening' and it transpires that this rose sent out what is known as a sport or mutation in Czechoslovakia and it was given the name 'Awakening'. To all intents and purposes the growing plant resembles its parent. The flower is the only difference. It has medium-sized double blooms which are bright pink at first and they are nicely fragrant. They are quartered and produced profusely.

BABY FAURAX

Raised by *Lille*
Parentage *Unknown*
Introduced *1924*
Type *Polyantha*
Size *60 x 60cm*

'Baby Faurax' is a lovely colour break in small-growing old roses, and provides excellent colour contrast. The small, quite double flowers are in clusters, lavender-purple in colour, pinking a little with age. This little beauty never fails to excite comment from those who see it for the first time. In truth, many of the old dwarf Polyanthas more than hold their own with the more modern Miniature and Patio roses.

BALLERINA

Raised by *Bentall*
Parentage *Unknown*
Introduced *1937*
Type *Hybrid Musk*
Size *1m x 1m*

Here we have a most beautiful rose allowing for the accepted fact that modern roses are not now as popular as they used to be. This lovely rose has small flowers about 3–4cm across, single rosy-pink on the edge and white towards the centre with a light fragrance. The raiser of this rose is given as Bentall, who was of course the Rev. J. H. Pemberton's gardener. It was Pemberton who did much of the original work in the creation of the Hybrid Musks, and when he died much of his breeding material was left unattended. The story about Bentall taking over the nursery is unclear and it is quite possible that some of the roses credited to Bentall were actually Pemberton's.

IT IS IMPOSSIBLE
TO IMAGINE THE WORLD
WITHOUT THE ROSE,

FOR IT HAS BEEN
ADORNING THE EARTH
SINCE TIME IMMEMORIAL,

CHEERING MAN
FROM HIS EARLIEST YEARS

CLAUDIA BINELLI

1
BARONNE PRÉVOST

Raised by *Desprez*
Parentage *Unknown*
Introduced *1842*
Type *Hybrid Perpetual*
Size *1m x 1m*

An extremely beautiful rose that some would say belongs to another era, but nevertheless holds its place today. It has large quite double blooms, which are rose-pink or cerise-pink of even colouring. They are full flat across when open and nicely fragrant, with upright growth and the ability to keep flowering right through to the autumn. Its flowers are about 10–12cm in width. One of the best of its class.

2
BELLE AMOUR

Raiser and parentage *Unknown*
Introduced *1940*
Type *Alba*
Size *1.5m x 1.5m*

Although there is considerable doubt about the origin of this rose, it is no less a beautiful variety. Most people know that many roses were grown from seed in the fields of France in the early part of the nineteenth century, and this may be one of them. It has large blooms up to 10cm or more across, which are semi-double and cupped, and of an attractive pink with shades of salmon at times. They have a delicious fragrance and look very well among the grey-green foliage.

3
BELLE ISIS

Raised by *Parmentier*
Parentage *Unknown*
Introduced *1845*
Type *Gallica*
Size *1m*

This is one of the early roses that inspired David Austin to launch his hybridising programme of breeding new roses that looked old and had the ability to keep on flowering. In its own right it is an extremely beautiful rose, having very double small to medium blooms, which open flat and are flesh-pink. They are quite fragrant with what has been described as the scent of myrrh. It grows into an attractive, tidy, tough plant, which is summer-flowering only. It will now, of course, always have a place in rose history because with 'Dainty Maid' it shares the parenthood of 'Constance Spry', the founding rose of the David Austin dynasty.

1	2
3	

BELLE STORY

Raised by *David Austin*
Parentage *('Chaucer' x 'Parade')*
x ('The Prioress' x 'Iceberg')
Introduced *1984*
Type *English Rose*
Size *1.5m x 1m*

Although this is one of David Austin's early productions it is a rose of extreme beauty. To watch the development and unfolding of this variety when we first received it was, to say the least, quite exciting and breathtaking. The buds, of course, look like many other roses and you have no prior warning of the beauty about to unfold before your eyes. The flower develops from a fat bud and opens cupped to a semi-double form of incurved petals, and when wide open it bravely displays a group of golden stamens. There are several shades of pink in the flower, which under certain conditions can have an iridescent sheen about it. The fragrance is strong and pleasant.

BLANC DOUBLE DE COUBERT

Raised by Cochet-Cochet
Parentage R. rugosa
x 'Sombreuil'
Introduced 1892
Type Hybrid Rugosa
Size 2m x 2m

Many people have not yet developed a love for the Rugosa family of roses but when they do they will not regret widening their appreciation into an extremely interesting family. This particular member can be of large proportions. The attractive dark green foliage is always healthy and sets off the large 10cm blooms, which are silky-white and loosely double. They are deliciously fragrant and can be followed by orange fruit, though not usually in great density. This is a classic Rugosa, growing into a magnificent shrub that can be used in many ways. It is an ideal evergreen shrub and makes an excellent untrained hedge.

BLANCHE MOREAU

Raised by Moreau-Robert
Parentage 'Comtesse de Murinais'
x 'Quatre Saisons Blanc Mousseux'
Introduced 1880
Type Moss
Size 1m

A lax-growing Moss rose of considerable importance. Not many white Moss roses have survived from the early period and this example is important for that reason. It has nicely fragrant medium-sized pure white flowers, which have a backing of brown bristly moss and fine prickles all over the stems.

BLUSH NOISETTE

Raised by Phillipe Noisette
Parentage Seedling from 'Champneys Pink Cluster'
Introduced 1817
Type Noisette
Size 4m or more

The Noisette group originated with Phillipe Noisette in a South Carolina nursery just after the turn of the nineteenth century and was increased by some seedlings sent to his brother, Louis, at his nursery near Paris. The group as a whole has quite complicated parentage coming from Bourbons, Teas, Chinas, and others but at the same time are one of the most varied groups available to gardeners around the world. This rose is one of the well-known ones. It has smallish 4cm blooms in large clusters, set in attractive glossy-green foliage. The flowers are rose-pink in the bud opening to pink and white and are quite flat with a pleasant scent.

1
BLYTHE SPIRIT

Raised by *David Austin*
Parentage *Unknown*
Introduced *1999*
Type *English Rose*
Size *1.5m x 1.5m*

One of the newest of the Austin roses. Its medium to large blooms are a good yellow at first, lightening a little with age. They are semi-double and have a pleasing fragrance while the sturdy plant has proved to be totally disease-resistant. At this time its parentage is not known but one must suspect that it comes from that most excellent rose, 'Graham Thomas'.

	2	3
1	---	---
	4	5

2
BOBBIE JAMES

Raised by *Sunningdale*
Parentage *R. Multiflora seedling*
Introduced *1960*
Type *Rambler*
Size *9m x 6m*

One of the most rampant and beautiful rambling roses you could ever come across but if you wish to plant it you must have a position where it can flourish untouched. It will easily cover a large shed, a tank stand, a large tree or even up 3 or 4 storeys of a building. You cannot imagine how beautiful this rose can be. It has massive heads of semi-double flowers, creamy white with a delicious penetrating fragrance that envelops everything near it. Named for the honourable Robert James, it was found as a chance seedling and has one summer-flowering season only.

3
BOTZARIS

Raiser and parentage *Unknown*
Introduced *1856*
Type *Damask*
Size *1m x 1m*

When we read about the classical old roses, mention is often made of such roses as 'Fantin-Latour', 'Maiden's Blush', 'Madame Hardy', and 'Charles de Mills'. 'Botzaris' deserves to be ranked among these old beauties for several reasons. The flower is flat across the top, is quartered, and comes from a fat pinkish bud, developing into a large 10–12cm quite double creamy-white bloom sometimes showing a green eye. It has a lovely scent and flowers all over a compact plant, with mid-green foliage, in the summer only. It is quite hardy and really is one of the most beautiful old roses. I saw it first in the magnificent garden of the late Valdemar Petersen of Löve, Denmark.

4
BOULE DE NEIGE

Raised by *Lacharmé*
Parentage *'Blanche Lafitte' x 'Sappho'*
Introduced *1867*
Type *Bourbon*
Size *1m x 1m*

This rose, although beautiful in several ways, can be difficult to succeed with and, given its parents of a Tea rose and an Alba, it should be much stronger. It has deep-green foliage among which appear exquisite double, white, cupped blooms, which are nicely fragrant. It can flower for a long period in the summer but does seem to object to very cold winters.

5
BREDON

Raised by *David Austin*
Parentage *'Wife of Bath' x 'Lilian Austin'*
Introduced *1984*
Type *English Rose*
Size *1m x 1m*

David Austin is and will be the raiser of some very different and beautiful roses and 'Bredon' is definitely one of them. In time its worth will be recognised. It flowers freely over a long period and forms a compact tidy plant with blooms of an unusual colour: buffy yellow or perhaps biscuit colour deeper towards the centre and paling towards the edges. They are 7–8cm across, quite flat and almost a perfect rosette formation made up of many small petals. Densely covered in flowers the plant is a sight to behold. It may also be used as a hedge.

BROTHER CADFAEL

Raised by *David Austin*
Parentage *'Charles Austin' x seedling*
Introduced *1990*
Type *English Rose*
Size *1.5m x 1.5m*

'Sumptuous' or 'voluptuous' could be the best words to describe this rose, which can have huge flowers at times. It has cupped blooms, which can remain nicely incurved as the flower opens. They are a nice shade of medium pink deepening to orange-pink in the centre and are possessed of quite a strong perfume.

BUFF BEAUTY

Raised by *Ann Bentall*
Parentage *'William Allen Richardson' x seedling*
Introduced *1939*
Type *Hybrid Musk*
Size *2m*

For about fifty years this rose has been available to gardeners all over the world but at the same time has been quite a mystery. With the passage of time, fresh information has been made available and it now appears that the credit for its creation goes to Ann Bentall, wife of the late Rev. J. H. Pemberton's gardener. It is a superb rose of a beautiful shade of buff-apricot, deepest in colour at opening and paler later. The attractive dark foliage looks well with the large blooms of about 8cm across. It has a lovely fragrance.

IF LOVE WERE
WHAT THE ROSE IS,

AND I WERE LIKE
THE LEAF,

OUR LIVES WOULD
GROW TOGETHER

IN SAD OR
SINGING
WEATHER

A. C. SWINBURNE, 1837–1909

1
CAMAIEUX

Raised by *Vibert*
Parentage *Unknown*
Introduced *1830*
Type *Gallica*
Size *1m*

One could probably think of seven or eight striped roses in the old rose families, and 'Camaieux' would probably be best known of all of them. There was a time when it was suggested that a virus caused the striping but exhaustive tests in California some years ago proved this to be incorrect. This beautiful rose probably has the widest stripes of all. The plant is reasonably compact and has mid-green foliage. Under good conditions the blooms can be about 10cm across. They come from plump buds and are loosely double. Basically the colour is white, heavily overlaid with stripes of pink and crimson. The colours are at their sharpest when the flower is freshly open and later the pink and crimson become lilac and mauve as the blooms age. They are also nicely scented.   ←—

2
CAMEO

Raised by *de Ruiter*
Parentage *'Orléans Rose' sport*
Introduced *1932*
Type *Polyantha*
Size *1m x 1m*

There was a period of time when Polyantha roses reigned supreme and it may be that the popular Miniature and Patio roses of today owe their early relatives a vote of thanks for their creation. After World War II, I remember packing quite large groups of Polyantha roses for distribution to other retailers. This variety has fresh salmon-coloured rosette flowers up to 5cm across. They are produced profusely and make a great display when in full flower. The blooms assemble in large clusters, which weigh the branches down. They have a light scent and pale a little with age but will not lose their colour when grown in the shade. Foliage is light green on a sturdy plant.

3
CARDINAL DE RICHELIEU

Raised by *Laffay*
Parentage *Unknown*
Introduced *1840*
Type *Gallica*
Size *1m*

Probably the darkest member of this family. There is some doubt about its classification but that does not stop this fine rose being well sought after. This is one old rose that benefits from a good cutting back and the removal of dead wood. The blooms are a deep dusky purplish-crimson, quite fragrant and about 6–8cm across. They are cupped when open and flat across the top and tend to become a mauvish-purple with age. Whereas most Gallicas have a number of small thorns on slim stems, this rose has few thorns at all.

4
CARDINAL HUME

Raised by *Harkness*
Parentage *Seedling x 'Frank Naylor'*
Introduced *1984*
Type *Shrub*
Size *1m x 1m*

A fairly new introduction with a fairly old look about it. The colour of the blooms is not far removed from the Gallica 'Tuscany Superb', being royal purple deepening with age. They are of small to medium size with the petals getting smaller towards the centre. Quite a few golden stamens stand out in the middle and they are nicely scented.

It could be said that liking striped roses is an acquired taste, much the same as eating kiwifruit or cucumber, but once you appreciate their benign beauty you will surely become hooked on their charms and will probably return to their festive table for more and more. Trevor Griffiths

1
CÉCILE BRÜNNER

Raised by *Pernet-Ducher*
Parentage *R. multiflora x 'Mme de Tartas'*
Introduced *1881*
Type *Polyantha*
Size *Over 1m*

This rose has stood the test of time with great distinction. It has been a magnificent rose from the time of its introduction – over a hundred years ago – and has come to be well known and respected. The only rose that surpasses this little beauty is the climbing form of 'Cécile Brünner'. There has been some confusion between this rose and one or two others, partly because growers continually propagate the wrong variety. 'Cécile Brünner' has pale pink beautifully formed small double flowers produced all over the plant. They are fragrant and could be described as a miniature Hybrid Tea. The plant develops into a compact tidy specimen, which is probably where it differs from imposters. Three other colours are available.

2
CELESTIAL

Raised by *Unknown*
Parentage *Alba Hybrid*
Introduced *Before 1848*
Type *Alba*
Size *2m*

In every family group of roses there are two or three specimens that are well known and revered around the world. It would not be incorrect to classify this rose as one of them. The blooms are a unique shade of silver-pink; in fact some have suggested that this rose is the origin of the term 'celestial pink'. They are about 10cm wide and are cupped but quite flat across the top. They are semi-double and open to show golden stamens in the centre. The iridescent shade of pink contrasts well with the greyish foliage, and all this coupled with an upright plant is a joy to see. It has a beautiful scent.

3
CHAPLIN'S PINK CLIMBER

Raised by *Chaplin*
Parentage *'Paul's Scarlet' x 'American Pillar'*
Introduction *1928*
Type *Climber*
Size *4m*

The blooms are a bright cerise-pink and sometimes there is a white line or two on the centre petals. This is a very tough rose that will grow where most others would not survive. The healthy, glossy deep-green foliage sets off the floral effort and the plant is literally covered with blossoms. Each flower is about 8cm across and semi-double, opening flat to show a good crop of gold stamens. Although this variety is summer-flowering only, it certainly attracts attention for the duration of its display.

4
CHARLES AUSTIN

Raised by *David Austin*
Parentage *'Aloha' x 'Chaucer'*
Introduced *1973*
Type *English Rose*
Size *2m*

In the early days of David Austin's hybridising programme, he used the rose 'Aloha' because of its obvious attributes. 'Charles Austin' was one of the products of this programme. It is a very fine rose, quite able to hold its own against the more recent English Roses. It can be rather tall in its growth and in many parts of our country is used as a climber to cover a trellis or a wooden fence. The blooms are large, up to 13cm across, quite double and have a strong fruity fragrance. They are flat and open to a deep apricot-orange paling later to a lighter shade, sometimes tinged with pink.

1	2
3	4

5
CHARLES DE MILLS

Raiser, parentage and introduction
Unknown
Type *Gallica*
Size *Up to 2m*

One of the loveliest and most popular of the Gallicas. It is a shame so little is known about it but at least it has survived for us to enjoy today. When it is growing in nursery rows it is quite distinct even without its flowers. The young plants are upright with slim stems and light green foliage, and when the large voluptuous blooms arrive it does not take long for their weight to force the branches downward. The flowers are all of 10cm wide and are tightly packed with petals. The blooms are flat and very fragrant and really do look as if they might have been trimmed flat with a pair of scissors.

6
CHARLOTTE

Raised by *David Austin*
Parentage *Seedling x 'Graham Thomas'*
Introduced *1993*
Type *English Rose*
Size *1.5m*

A favourite rose of David Austin himself, and it is easy to see that it comes from 'Graham Thomas'. It is a softer yellow and cupped in shape and the blooms are produced with great freedom over a long flowering season. It is graced with a delicious Tea Rose fragrance and has glossy foliage on a healthy plant.

7
CHAUCER

Raised by *David Austin*
Parentage *'Duchesse de Montebello'*
x 'Constance Spry'
Introduced *1970*
Type *English Rose*
Size *1m*

When this rose was first introduced, those of us who were new to English Roses could never have imagined what was to follow. But looking back now, 'Chaucer' blazed the trail for them all. I have no doubt that had Geoffrey Chaucer been able to see this rose he would have been very proud of it. It has medium-sized double flowers, bright pink in the middle and paling towards the edge. They are cupped, quartered and very fragrant. The plant grows to about 1m and can be covered in blooms. Both parents are summer-flowering only and yet they have produced the recurrent-flowering variety 'Chaucer'.

8
CITY OF YORK

Raised by *Tantau*
Parentage *'Professor Gnau' x 'Dorothy Perkins'*
Introduced *1945*
Type *Climber*
Size *3m*

A very beautiful summer-flowering low climber, which has large blooms that open flat and wide with the stamens showing. It has creamy-white flowers set in dark glossy-green healthy foliage. They are delightfully fragrant and are prolifically produced during its long flowering season. A point to remember is that roses that have a summer-flowering season only usually fit neatly into the break that twice-flowering Climbers or Ramblers have.

5	6
7	8

CLAIRE JACQUIER

Raised by *Bernaix*
Parentage *Unknown*
Introduced *1888*
Type *Noisette*
Size *7–8m*

CLAIRE ROSE

Raised by *David Austin*
Parentage *'Charles Austin' x*
('seedling' x 'Iceberg')
Introduced *1986*
Type *English Rose*
Size *1m x 1m*

COMMON MOSS

Raiser and parentage *Unknown*
Introduced *Prior to 1700*
Type *Moss*
Size *1m*

Here we have another example of the beautiful and exciting Noisette family. This deep yellow rose came to my attention when I first met David Steen, husband of the late Nancy Steen – one of New Zealand's experts on old roses. David wore one in the buttonhole of his suit every day he went to the office, which proves that this variety, grown in the warmer parts of New Zealand, can flower for most of the year. Sometimes it is confused as a yellow form of 'Cécile Brünner'. It has very vigorous growth, excellent foliage, and clusters of small, double, deep yellow flowers that are deliciously scented. It is an excellent climbing rose for many purposes.

A fine example of the English Rose family, which does very well when it gets a situation to suit it. In many ways 'Claire Rose' is reminiscent of 'Souvenir de la Malmaison'. They are a similar colour, although 'Claire Rose' has many more petals. They both tend to spot during bad weather and both can ball under similar conditions. At first the blooms of 'Claire Rose' have a little pale orange-apricot in the centre, then they become blush-pink and then pale to cream. The flowers are large, perfectly formed, very double and fragrant. The growth is upright with light green foliage. While mentioning the similarity of some English Roses to Bourbons, it seems certain they will also supersede them.

Summer-flowering only, this is considered to be the original Moss rose, and its history is not known. The buds are lightly mossed or covered with prickles while the flowers are clear pink, quite double and sweetly scented. The plant growth is rather lax, added to by the weight of the blooms. Requires staking.

These roses always have been and I hope always will be favourites; for what can be more elegant than the bud of the Moss rose, with its pure rose colour, peeping through that beautiful and unique envelope. Thomas Rivers

COMPLICATA

Origin, parentage and introduction *Unknown*
Type *Included in the Gallicas*
Size *2m*

This rose is an enigma in several ways. By rights it does not belong to the Gallicas at all and one has to wonder how it ever arrived there. It has quite smooth stems and quite large foliage, contrary to most of the Gallicas. As if this is not enough, the flower is totally different too. The large single blooms are bright rose-pink with a lighter centre. The name is a contradiction as well, there being nothing complicated about this rose at all.

COMTE DE CHAMBORD

Raised by *Robert and Mareau*
Parentage *Unknown*
Introduced *1860*
Type *Portland*
Size *1m*

Sadly this rose belongs to the family that lasted in popularity only a short time and was swept aside by the brash Hybrid Perpetuals. I say sadly because there were some very beautiful varieties in the Portlands, which really were not appreciated as they should have been. Nevertheless a nice group of them has survived to remind us that this was the first family to have the ability to flower again. 'Comte de Chambord' has a very double bloom reminiscent of an English Rose, and if it has a fault at all it lies in the flower being rather deeply set in the mid-green foliage. The blooms are full-petalled opening quartered and flat, are nicely fragrant, and are a warm, rich pink in colour.

CORNELIA

Raised by *Pemberton*
Parentage *Unknown, possibly from 'Lessing'*
Introduced *1925*
Type *Hybrid Musk*
Size *2m*

It seems that the parentage of 'Cornelia' is not known, but perhaps one day it might present itself. There is no doubt in my mind that 'Lessing', a Hybrid Musk raised by Peter Lambert in 1914, may have had quite a lot to do with it. 'Lessing' comes from 'Trier' x 'Entente Cordiale' and when examined closely it has a strong resemblance to 'Cornelia'. This variety is one of a small group of roses of this type that have been very popular, mostly because they have had so much written about them. It is my prediction that many others now being discovered by astute gardeners will become better known in the future. 'Cornelia' has lovely stems covered in a mass of small, double pink and apricot blooms. They are about 4cm across and have a lovely fragrance. The plant can grow quite tall and is suitable as a climber or a hedge. It flowers over a long period.

AND THE BEST AND
THE WORST OF THIS
IS THAT NEITHER
IS MOST TO BLAME,

IF YOU HAVE
FORGOTTEN MY KISSES
AND I HAVE FORGOTTEN
YOUR NAME

A. C. SWINBURNE, 1837–1909

COTTAGE ROSE

Raised by David Austin
Parentage 'Wife of Bath'
x 'Mary Rose'
Introduced 1991

Type English Rose
Size 1m

This variety is one of the smallest growing of the group, reaching perhaps 1m or less high, which makes it ideal for a small garden. The healthy, upright plant supports medium-sized cupped rosettes of an even, bright pink. Slightly scented, they flower from early in the season until autumn.   *opposite* →

68

CRESTED MOSS

Raised by *Vibert*
Parentage *Unknown*
Introduced *1827*
Type *Moss*
Size *1m*

A most unusual rose, more familiarly known as 'Chapeau de Napoleon' or 'Napoleon's Hat'. On the sepals at the back of the buds are peculiar excrescences or mossing, which really do look like an old triangular hat. The flowers are double, bright clear pink and scented.

CRIMSON SHOWER

Raised by *Norman*
Parentage *Seedling from 'Excelsa'*
Introduced *1951*
Type *Rambler*
Size *Up to 5m*

The creation of this rose, by intention or otherwise, was a happy coincidence because up to the date of its introduction other red ramblers, although they provided adequate displays, did not have the ability to flower again later. Each bloom of about 3cm forms a rosette of deep crimson; they appear in large clusters and have a light scent. The flowers commence late in the season but also continue late. All things considered, this is a beautiful and useful rambler, which is also used for weeping standards.

COUPE D'OR

Raised by *Barbier*
Parentage *'Jacotte' seedling*
Introduced *1930*
Type *Rambler*
Size *3m x 3m*

Now and again a rose arrives on the scene that really excites the genuine enthusiast. This is one of them. The flowers are about 5–6cm across, very double, quartered and fragrant. They appear in clusters and are palish-yellow to mid-yellow and are supported by leathery dark green foliage on a healthy plant. At first sight this variety can only excite the purist with its pretty colour shadings and its obviously old-type flower and sweet scent. A little gem.

CRÉPUSCULE

Raised by *Dubreuil*
Parentage *Probably from 'William Allen Richardson'*
Introduced *1904*
Type *Noisette*
Size *4m x 4m*

This is a comparatively unknown rose, which I had the pleasure of introducing into New Zealand from my old friend, the late Valdemar Petersen of Denmark. Although its parentage is obscure, it may have come from 'William Allen Richardson' as at times it bears quite a resemblance. The plant will climb or can be trained as a shrub. In either case, it covers itself with a great density of blossom in a very attractive shade of orange-apricot. The blooms are semi-double, fragrant, deeper in the centre and lighter towards the edges. The light green foliage, deep reddish-brown young shoots and few thorns are some of the attractive features of this popular rose.

CROWN PRINCESS MARGARETA

Raised by *David Austin*
Parentage *Unknown as yet*
Introduced *1999*
Type *English Rose*
Size *1.5m x 1.5m*

A new release from Austin of England, this rose is very beautiful and bound to become popular because of its lovely colour and fragrance. It is tall growing and has arching branches, which are accentuated by the clusters of very double orange-apricot blooms that can be quite heavy. They are heavily laden with a strong fruity fragrance, while the plant is tough and hardy and should do well in most situations.

following page →

1	2
3	4

1
DAINTY BESS

Raised by *Archer*
Parentage *'Ophelia' x 'Kitchener of Khartoum'*
Introduced *1925*
Type *Hybrid Tea*
Size *1m*

Single roses, that is, those with only five petals, have not been generally popular but when one develops a taste for them usually the desire for more grows in an alarming manner. This exquisite rose has only five petals and, when the flower is open, the large boss of purplish-crimson stamens is quite prominent. The colour is deeper pink on the outside and silver-pink on the inside, and the flowers are large, up to 13cm across. It has upright growth and a strong fresh scent, and also exists in a lovely climbing form.

2
DAPPLE DAWN

Raised by *David Austin*
Parentage *Sport from 'Red Coat'*
Introduced *1983*
Type *English Rose*
Size *1.5m*

A prolific flowering rose that grows into a nice rounded shrub covered over a long season with large, lightly scented blooms at least 13cm across. Each bloom has five petals and a few petaloids and prominent stamens. The colour is a pretty silvery-pink lightening in the centre.

3
DESPREZ À FLEUR JAUNE

Raised by *Desprez*
Parentage *'Blush Noisette' x 'Parks' Yellow Tea-Scented China'*
Introduced *1830*
Type *Noisette*
Size *5m or more*

An excitingly beautiful and different rose. Of all the roses that have passed through my hands in over fifty years of working with them, this one has a fragrance that is different from all others. It is difficult to describe: haunting, delicious, fruity, powerful and all pervading. This rose also has the ability to remain in flower almost continuously. It will cover a huge area and its pretty, light green foliage sets off the lemon-pink, double blooms, which are about 5cm across. At times shades of yellow and pale apricot and pink appear in the blooms. An unusual feature of this plant's growth is the angular turn of each node on the stems.

4
DEVONIENSIS

Raised by *Pavitt*
Parentage *Sport from 'Tea Devoniensis'*
Introduced *1858*
Type *Climbing Tea Rose*
Size *4m*

This lovely old climbing Tea Rose is often referred to as the 'Magnolia Rose'. Because of its large flowers and particularly because of its creamy-white colour, it shows up well against the wall of a dark-stained house or fence. The blooms have an attractive flush of apricot deep down in the centre when they first open. They have a strong Tea fragrance and the plant flowers recurrently.

DOROTHY PERKINS

Raised by *Jackson and Perkins*
Parentage *R. wichuraiana*
x 'Mme Gabriel Luizot'
Introduced *1901*
Type *Rambler*
Size *5m or more*

Because this rose has been on the scene for a long time it seems older than its introduction date. Its only drawback seems to be that it has only one summer-flowering season. However, this flowering can be a joy to behold. The blooms are about 3–4cm in width and form in large clusters, which in turn are very close to other clusters, the whole creating a mass, colourful display of rich salmon-pink. This is the rose that can be seen all over the world growing unattended in the most difficult and neglected situations.

DORTMUND

Raised by *Kordes*
Parentage *Seedling x R. kordesii*
Introduced *1955*
Type *Shrub-climber*
Size *3–4m*

The house of Kordes in Germany has produced hundreds of beautiful hardy roses through four generations of the Kordes family. Without a doubt every rose in this volume could have come from this industrious and successful firm of rose hybridisers. It would be easy to say, 'Why has such-and-such a rose not been included?' 'Dortmund' is here because of its influence on hybridisers of all countries and of course the fact that it appears in the pedigree of many roses. It has deep green, glossy foliage, clean, prickly growth and overall is very healthy. The almost single flowers are large (12cm) bright scarlet-crimson with white in the throat, and when open the stamens show up well. It has a long flowering period.

DUC DE GUICHE

Raiser *Prevost*
Parentage *Unknown*
Introduced *Prior to 1838*
Type *Gallica*
Size *1.5m*

It is a well-known fact that the early French and Belgian rose growers did not carry out hybridising in the sophisticated manner in which it is carried out today. The growers of some two hundred years ago simply sowed rose seed gathered from mature plants in rows in the field and selected the most interesting new seedlings to increase for the future. This rose could easily have originated that way. The beautifully formed blooms are of classical Gallica shape. They are medium to large in size and open very double, quartered and flat across the top, and are a rich purplish-crimson, lighter on the edges and with a sharp fragrance.

Duchesse D'Angoulême →

DUCHESSE D'ANGOULÊME

Raiser *Vibert*
Parentage *Unknown*
Introduced *1827*
Type *Gallica*
Size *1m*

Vibert and his family were close friends of Pierre-Joseph Redouté, and the two families spent a great deal of time together. Redouté was known as the 'man who painted roses' and Vibert as 'a man who created beautiful roses'. 'Duchesse d'Angoulême' was one of them and was affectionately called 'the wax flower'. It has almost translucent pink blooms that are globular in the bud, cupped on opening, quite double and with a fragrance. The large flowers tend to hang down on the plant, which is summer-flowering only.

← *previous page*

DUCHESSE DE BRABANT

Raiser *Bernède*
Parentage *Unknown*
Introduction *1857*
Type *Tea Rose*
Size *1m*

Many hundreds of Tea Roses were created by many rose growers and hybridisers. However, perhaps only a small number of them have survived to the present day. It would be correct to say that only those with the best constitutions in most situations would survive. 'Duchesse de Brabant' is one of these survivors. The double blooms are a soft rosy-pink, large cupped and very fragrant. The spreading, wiry growth of the plant is typical of the family.

DUCHESSE DE MONTEBELLO

Raiser *Laffay*
Parentage *Unknown*
Introduced *1829*
Type *Gallica*
Size *1.5m*

Some enthusiasts would consider this variety one of the prettiest of the Gallicas, if not one of the best of the old roses. The shell-pink colour of the flowers is quite exquisite. The fat buds open to cupped blooms that are quartered, quite flat across the top, have a rolled centre, a green eye, and are sweetly fragrant. What more could one ask? Some years ago, on a visit to a contract grower in California, I was surprised to find that the name of his business was the Montebello Rose Company. On being asked if he knew the beautiful Gallica 'Duchesse de Montebello', the answer was in the negative – another surprise.

DUPONTII

Raiser and parentage *Unknown*
Introduced *1817*
Type *Species Hybrid*
Size *3m x 2m*

Summer-flowering only with large creamy-white single flowers, which have a lovely fragrance and are about 8cm across. Sometimes they are tinged with pink and have a nice group of golden-yellow stamens. They sit very well on a large plant among the grey-green foliage.

When roses are described to gardeners as summer or once-flowering only, it is sometimes amazing to see their reaction, and yet those same people usually have gardens full of azaleas, camellias and rhododendrons, which of course are once-flowering and probably have less of a season than the summer-flowering roses. Trevor Griffiths

1
EASLEA'S GOLDEN RAMBLER

Raiser *Easlea*
Parentage *Unknown*
Introduced *1932*
Type *Rambler*
Size *3–4m*

A rather beautiful climber or rambler that does not seem so popular today. Summer-flowering only, this variety has large blooms up to at least 10cm or more, which are a buffy-gold, sometimes with scarlet appearing as marks on the petals. It may flower but once a season but its fragrance is sweet, strong and pervading.

2
EGLANTYNE

Raised by *David Austin*
Parentage *'Giant Meyeri' x 'Mary Rose'*
Introduced *1994*
Type *English Rose*
Size *1.5m*

If you had to choose one English Rose for your garden, this rose, 'Eglantyne', could be your choice. It is a magnificent rose in every way, with upright, healthy growth, and foliage that suffers very little from pests and diseases. The blooms are large and exquisitely formed, cupped at first, opening out flat, and are quartered with a rolled centre. The clear medium-pink colour matches the delicious fragrance. It bears the Christian name of the lady who founded the Save the Children Fund during World War I.

← *page 81*

3
ELMSHORN

Raised by *Kordes*
Parentage *'Hamburg' x 'Verdeen'*
Introduced *1951*
Type *Shrub*
Size *2m*

Planted in the shrubbery this different variety could be just the rose to brighten up a dull area. Growing to a large shrub, the plant is adorned with large clusters of small 3cm blooms of bright deep pink, which are slightly fragrant. They are produced more or less continuously and are set in light green foliage.

4
EMILY GRAY

Raised by *Williams*
Parentage *'Jersey Beauty' x 'Comtesse du Cayla'*
Introduced *1918*
Type *Rambler*
Size *4–5m*

A beauty from another era, this rose is still sought after today. The colour of the blooms is not common among roses and is a deep buffy-orange backed by dark young foliage. As the foliage ages it becomes deep glossy-green, and the whole presents a glorious picture of colour and tranquillity. The flowers are large, have up to twenty-five petals, and are fragrant.

ENGLISH GARDEN

Raised by *David Austin*
Parentage *('Lilian Austin'*
x seedling) x ('Iceberg'
x 'Wife of Bath')
Introduced *1986*
Type *English Rose*
Size *1m*

One often wonders about the naming of a rose and the reasons for the decision. Perhaps as lovers of roses we think that we can do better. However, in this case the name seems to be particularly appropriate, as one can see these lovely blooms melding themselves into an English garden so well that passersby may not even realise that the plant is a rose. The individual blooms are at least 10cm across and during the opening process are lovely rosettes, later having a more muddled centre. The colour is at first buffy-yellow, paling with age to creamy-white and lemon at the edges. This is one of the smaller-growing English Roses and has a lovely Tea scent.

ERFURT

Raised by *Kordes*
Parentage *'Eva' x 'Réveil Dijonnais'*
Introduced *1939*
Type *Hybrid Musk*
Size *Up to 2m*

When the name of this rose is mentioned I am immediately reminded of my first visit to East Germany in 1984. As a lone traveller there were many obstacles placed in my way and without the help of a drunk Russian my difficulties could have been far greater. However, 'Erfurt' the rose is very beautiful and gardeners in all countries are just beginning to appreciate its many attributes. The foliage is tough and leathery and the young growth is quite dark and bronzy. The flowers are very fragrant, semi-double and basically lemon-white with a rosy carmine edge. Probably 12cm across, they appear in clusters on long, strong stems that could easily be made to climb. There is an almost continuous display.

ÉTOILE DE HOLLANDE

Raised by *Leenders*
Parentage *Climbing sport*
Introduced *1931*
Type *Climber*
Size *Up to 5m*

Over the years many climbing roses have originated from climbing sports of bush roses and this would be one of the best to come forward by this method. There are always comments about such red climbing roses as 'Guinée', 'Birthday Present', 'Crimson Glory', and more recently 'Dublin Bay', all of which have inherent faults. But these faults are not present in 'Étoile de Hollande'. It has large, loosely double blooms of the deepest crimson and has a very strong Damask scent. An excellent climber when established.

Evelyn $\longrightarrow$

EUPHRATES

Raised by *Harkness*
Parentage *R. persica x 'Fairy Changeling'*
Introduced *1986*
Type *Shrub*
Size *1m*

Most breeding houses over the passage of time settle on one or two base varieties from which they develop their breeding programme. In this case the rose chosen was *R. persica* or, more correctly, *Hulthemia persica,* which is so closely related to the rose genus that it will cross breed with the family fairly easily. The flowers are small at about 3cm, single, and are of a most unusual colour – probably pinkish-mauve would best describe them. They have a purplish-crimson blotch at the base of each petal and prominent stamens. The foliage is Hulthemia-like.

EVELYN

Raiser *David Austin*
Parentage *'Graham Thomas' x 'Tamora'*
Introduced *1991*
Type *English Rose*
Size *1m*

'Evelyn' is considered to be the most fragrant rose produced by David Austin. It has large blooms at 15cm across and they are produced freely on a sturdy plant. If it has a fault at all it lies in the soft young growth, which seems to break easily. However, the flowers are unforgettably large in every sense of the word. They are of colours a little difficult to describe: peach, lemon, buff, bronze, apricot and pink all appear in the flowers at different times.

 ← previous page

EYEOPENER

Raised by *Interplant*
Parentage *(Seedling x 'Eyepaint') x (seedling x 'Dortmund')*
Introduced *1987*
Type *Procumbent*
Size *1m*

In recent times the term 'ground-cover' has been used to describe many roses, but I believe, like Peter Beales, the word to describe them is 'procumbent' because they are not evergreen. This rose was one of the forerunners in this class and is extremely attractive, with its arching branches literally covered with clusters of crimson-scarlet smallish blooms with yellow centres. It is long-flowering with a bright display.

The rose 'Evelyn' is a good example of hybridisers using a rose to fund their breeding programme, and in this case it was the English company of perfumers and toiletries, Crabtree & Evelyn, who bought the rights to the rose. They not only achieved the right to name the rose, they also went much further and used the perfume in the creation of a new range of perfume, body lotion, soap, bath cubes, talcum powder and deodorant, etc, and apparently their decision to do so has been very successful.

FAIR BIANCA

Raised by *David Austin*
Parentage *Unknown*
Introduced *1982*
Type *English Rose*
Size *1m*

Everyone who knows the beautiful Damask 'Mme Hardy' will be interested in this excellent addition to the English Roses. At first sight it is similar to 'Mme Hardy', but a closer examination reveals several differences. It does not grow into such a large plant, reaching about 1m in height. The flowers are a little creamy at first, becoming pure white with age. They are cupped, filled with many petals, and quartered, and when fully open have a button eye and green centre. Strongly scented of myrrh, this rose comes very close to the perfection of 'Mme Hardy' but has one major difference – its ability to flower on into the autumn.

FALSTAFF

Raised by *David Austin*
Parentage *Unknown as yet*
Introduced *1999*
Type *English Rose*
Size *1.5m*

Claimed by David Austin Roses to be the best red rose they have raised so far. From what I have seen of it so far it is truly beautiful. It has large cupped, full-petalled flowers of rich deep crimson. The flowers are at least 8–10cm across, nicely quartered and have a beautiful old rose fragrance. It grows into a handsome plant, healthy and upright.

opposite →

It may be part of the appeal of old garden roses that the truth about the history and provenance of other varieties will remain forever beyond our reach, lost in the gardens of the past. Peter Schneider

1	2
3	4

5	6
7	8

1
FANTIN-LATOUR

**Raiser, parentage and introduction
date** *Unknown*
Type *Centifolia*
Size *1.5m*

I always feel a little sad when discussing a rose such as this. Somewhere, sometime, someone knew everything about this beautiful, classical old rose, but modern researchers have been unable to discover the origins and story behind this very fine variety, loosely classified as a Centifolia. It is unfortunate that the information was not written down. It is suggested that the foliage shows a China influence although the blooms are more like a typical Centifolia. About 10cm wide, the flowers are pink to blush-pink and are nicely scented.

2
FELICIA

Raised by *Pemberton*
Parentage *'Trier' x 'Ophelia'*
Introduced *1928*
Type *Hybrid Musk*
Size *1.5m*

The Rev. J. H. Pemberton has been given the credit by some researchers for the creation of the Hybrid Musk group. While this may be true, Peter Lambert of Germany worked along similar lines with considerable success before Pemberton. It is significant that this rose came from 'Trier', one of Lambert's roses, and both 'Cornelia' and 'Penelope' have 'Trier' in their ancestry. 'Felicia' always impresses with its medium-sized (8cm) blooms, literally covering the healthy, compact plant. They open silver-pink with deeper shades in the centre, and have a strong fragrance and recurrency in performance.

3
FÉLICITÉ ET PERPÉTUE

Raised by *Jacques*
Parentage *R. sempervirens seedling*
Introduced *1827*
Type *Rambler*
Size *5m or more*

There are several stories relating to the naming of this rose and I choose to relate to you one of the oldest, leaving it to you, the reader, to decide which may or may not be the nearest to the truth. This rose was named for St Felicitas and St Perpetuas and was changed by Jacques, the French rose grower, to the more correct language of Félicité et Perpétue. These saints both have the same Saint's Day of May 7th. Irrespective of who is right and who is wrong, the rose itself is still well sought after even though it is over 170 years since its introduction. The blooms develop from small, fat, reddish buds into beautifully formed white rosettes about 4cm across. The attractive green foliage seems to be extremely healthy.

4
FÉLICITÉ PARMENTIER

Raised by *Parmentier*
Parentage *Unknown*
Introduced *1834*
Type *Alba*
Size *1m or more*

Once again we have an exquisite rose of which there appears to be no record. If Parmentier of Belgium was responsible for the introduction of the lovely Gallica 'Belle Isis', it seems quite feasible that he or one of his contemporaries was responsible for this rose too. It has rather more greenish foliage than the average Alba, and this may indicate that it is part Gallica. The buds are fat and open with a shade of lemon, soon changing to medium-pink as the flower opens, and then fading to blush-pink and white. They are almost 8cm wide, quartered, flat across the flower and very fragrant.

5
FELLEMBERG

Raiser and parentage *Unknown*
Introduced *1835*
Type *China*
Size *1m*

A lovely representative of the family, this rose has semi-double pink to crimson blooms of medium size. It has quite an ability to keep on flowering for long periods. In fact, a century later it could have been a Floribunda.

6
FERDINAND PICHARD

Raised by *Tanne*
Parentage *Unknown*
Introduced *1921*
Type *Hybrid Perpetual*
Size *Over 1m*

There are several old-type roses available today that are striped one way or the other and this variety is one of the best, both in colour and its ability to flower again and again during the summer and autumn. The pink blooms are striped quite clearly with purple and crimson, and are sweetly scented. The plant has vigorous growth and repeat blooming.

7
FERNAND TANNE

Raised by *Tanne*
Parentage *Unknown*
Introduced *1920*
Type *Rambler*
Size *5m*

It is sometimes said that many of the old Ramblers flower only once in summer but this is not true in many cases. Some varieties are described in European catalogues as summer-flowering only but when grown under New Zealand conditions have the ability to flower again and again. This very beautiful variety has fat, creamy buds opening to pale lemon and buff and deepening to apricot in the centres. The flowers are of medium size with many petals, which could be said to be laciniated in a mild way, and they possess a delicious strong fragrance. The lovely crop of blooms is set off by dark, healthy, strong foliage.

8
FORTUNE'S DOUBLE YELLOW

Raiser and parentage *Unknown*
Introduced *1845 by Robert Fortune*
Type *Climber*
Size *5m*

Because this rose is not hardy it is not grown successfully very often. But if you can succeed with it, it really is a joy to behold. More by good fortune than design we grew a plant on the north side of a concrete block shed where it could feel the cold of winter but was protected enough to survive and break into growth each spring. The blooms are large and light buff-yellow at first, changing to shades of peach and pink and apricot as the flower ages. It will grow into a magnificent specimen when placed in a favourable situation.

FRANCIS DUBREUIL

Raised by *Dubreuil*
Parentage *Unknown*
Introduced *1894*
Type *Tea Rose*
Size *1m*

FRANCOFURTANA

Raiser and parentage *Unknown*
Introduced *Before 1853*
Type *Gallica Hybrid*
Size *1m*

FRANÇOIS JURANVILLE

Raised by *Barbier*
Parentage *R. wichuraiana x*
'Mme Laurette Messimy'
Introduced *1906*
Type *Rambler*
Size *8–10m or more*

This rose came to my attention on a visit to the Sangerhausen Rosarium in East Germany in 1984. Its colour, scent and form stood out from others adjacent to it. The medium-sized blooms are quite blackish in the bud and open first to blackish-crimson, then pale to crimson as they age. They are quite double with a muddled centre and of course are nicely fragrant. The plant has an upright habit of growth and the flowers appear over a long period of time.

A beautiful old rose with an unknown past. The plant is compact with bushy growth and the flowers are large and a bright pink with loose wavy petals, sometimes veined deeper, followed by a crop of fruit. Unusual and distinctive.

Barbier of France was a prolific creator of roses and it was my pleasure to introduce many of his beautiful varieties to New Zealand. Surprisingly, this rose is sometimes mistaken for 'Albertine'. It has medium-sized blooms, about 10cm wide, with a strong apple fragrance. They are coral-pink on the outside and deeper towards the centre with lemon at the base of the petals. About the same period of time of introduction of this rose, Barbier produced three other beautiful Ramblers. These are 'François Foucard', which is lemon-yellow in colour and was introduced in 1900, 'François Poisson', introduced in 1907, with sulphur-yellow to white blooms, and 'François Guillot', which has lemon to milk-white blooms and also introduced in 1907.

FRAU DAGMAR HASTRUP

Raised by *Hastrup*
Parentage *Rugosa seedling*
Introduced *1914*
Type *Rugosa*
Size *1m*

FRED LOADS

Raised by *Holmes*
Parentage *'Orange Sensation' x 'Dorothy Wheatcroft'*
Introduced *1967*
Type *Shrub-climber*
Size *3–4m*

FRENSHAM

Raised by *Norman*
Parentage *Floribunda seedling x 'Crimson Glory'*
Introduced *1946*
Type *Floribunda*
Size *1m*

Europeans have shown the rest of the world how to use Rugosas, which are natives of Korea and Japan. When travelling by train, especially through countries such as Denmark and Germany, you can see members of the Rugosa group almost everywhere, showing amazing adaptability to natural and man-made environments alike. They are prominent around railway stations and embankments, industrial sites, and in and around motorway turnoffs and median strips. They are tough, and this variety is no exception. The large single blooms (10cm wide) are rose-pink with lemon-yellow stamens. Both fruit and flowers can be present on the plant at the same time. This is an excellent rose for hardy situations.

If you have a position in your garden that is a little dull and needs some height, this rose could be the plant to do the job for you. Our plant was growing against a two-storey building and when in flower it never failed to receive favourable comments. The quite large blooms (10cm wide) are almost single and are the clearest bright vermilion shade. They appear in large clusters and flower throughout summer and well into the autumn. Added to all this, they are nicely fragrant.

In every age there have been roses that are outstanding in their time and this is probably the reason why they have survived for us to enjoy today. 'Frensham' is one of these roses. For a rose to last in commerce and popularity for any length of time it must have special attributes. This rose arrived just at the end of World War II and it may have been its prominent deep crimson, semi-double, medium-sized blooms that took the imagination, but it became very popular for bedding roses all over the world. It has a light fragrance.

FRITZ NOBIS

Raised by *Kordes*
Parentage *'Joanna Hill' x 'Magnifica'*
Introduced *1940*
Type *Shrub-climber*
Size *Over 2m*

Although this rose is summer-flowering only, it still merits a place in every garden. It grows into a large rounded shrub, absolutely covered in flowers when at its peak. In England and Europe it is also grown as a climber. The long pointed buds are reddish, opening to a creamy pink with a salmon-pink underside – a beautiful combination of colour – and they are fragrant. The blooms are 9cm across and open flat and wide with stamens showing. A noble rose indeed.

FRÜHLINGSANFANG

Raised by *Kordes*
Parentage *'Joanna Hill' x R. spinosissima altaica*
Introduced *1950*
Type *Shrub-climber*
Size *2–3m*

Kordes produced eight magnificent roses in this group and 'Frühlingsanfang' is one of the lesser-known ones. It has large semi-double 12cm blooms, which are a creamy-ivory in colour and very fragrant. Mostly summer-flowering, there is a great profusion of blossom at its peak.

DON'T STREW ME
WITH ROSES AFTER
I'M DEAD,

WHEN DEATH CLAIMS
THE LIGHT OF
MY BROW,

NO FLOWERS OF LIFE
WILL CHEER ME:

INSTEAD YOU MAY
GIVE ME MY
ROSES NOW!

THOMAS F. HEALEY

FRÜHLINGSDUFT

Raised by *Kordes*
Parentage *'Joanna Hill'*
x R. spinosissima altaica
Introduced *1949*
Type *Shrub-climber*
Size *2–3m*

Large double flowers of at least 12cm wide grace a healthy, upright plant that would be a benefit in any larger garden. The flowers are the most fragrant of the group, borne out by its name, which translates into 'Fragrant Spring'. They are lemon-pink and apricot shades.

FRÜHLINGSGOLD

Raised by *Kordes*
Parentage *'Joanna Hill'*
x R. spinosissima hispida
Introduced *1937*
Type *Shrub-climber*
Size *2-3m*

This beautiful variety was the first in this series and is still popular for larger gardens. There are a number of obvious similarities in this group but because the *R. spinosissima* influence has been stronger than that of 'Joanna Hill', we have a tough, durable plant that quite literally grows anywhere. The flowers are large, about 13cm wide, and a pretty shade of medium golden-yellow. They are a little more than single and extremely fragrant. Like all the members of the Frühlings group, they flower early in the spring, when they have a massive display. The growth is upright and tall, the foliage is attractive, and fine prickles cover the stems.

FRÜHLINGSMORGEN

Raised by *Kordes*
Parentage *('E. G. Hill'*
x 'Catherine Kordes')
x R. spinosissima altaica
Introduced *1942*
Type *Shrub-climber*
Size *2-3m*

'Frühlings' means 'Spring' in German, and all in this group flower early, gaining the ability from the *R. spinosissima* collection. This variety has blooms that are large, 12cm, and single. Towards the edges they are deep rosy-pink and pale to lemon and white in the centre. The rest of the group are 'Frühlingsschnee', 'Frühlingstunde', 'Frühlingstag', and 'Frühlingszauber', which in their own way and in their own time are quite beautiful.

GEOFF HAMILTON

Raised by *David Austin*
Parentage *'Heritage'*
x unnamed seedling
Introduced *1997*
Type *English Rose*
Size *1.5m*

A 1997 release from David Austin Roses which is very much in keeping with other roses that have come from this creator. This is a strong-growing, healthy, and exceptionally disease-resistant rose. It is delicate in appearance, cupped at first, with the outer edge of the flower paling to white while the heart of the bloom is a warm, soft pink. It has a light old rose fragrance and is quartered.

 opposite

GEORG ARENDS

Raised by *Hinner*
Parentage *'Frau Karl Druschki' x 'La France'*
Introduced *1910*
Type *Hybrid Perpetual*
Size *1.5m*

With parents like this, 'Georg Arends' could hardly be anything other than a beautiful rose. The very fragrant, large blooms are medium-pink and nicely double. The Hybrid Perpetual group was previously very large and at the height of its popularity many hundreds existed. However, only a few have survived. 'Georg Arends' is one of the best.

GERTRUDE JEKYLL

Raised by *David Austin*
Parentage *'Wife of Bath' x 'Comte de Chambord'*
Introduced *1986*
Type *English Rose*
Size *2m*

This rose is named after one of the greatest landscape gardeners the world has ever seen and it seems right and proper to have such a magnificent rose to commemorate her name. It has an extremely good fragrance and has been chosen to be grown commercially to produce the first rose perfume in the United Kingdom for 250 years. When we saw the first bloom of this variety unfold, it was obvious that it was going to be well received. The large flowers are a rich, deep, bright pink, with the petals spiralling as they open.

GHISLAINE DE FÉLIGONDE

Raised by *Turbat*
Parentage *'Goldfinch' x unknown*
Introduced *1916*
Type *Hybrid Musk*
Size *3m or more*

The other parent for this rose is believed to be a Hybrid Musk, possibly 'Trier'. We had the pleasure of introducing this rose to New Zealand. It came from my late friend, Valdemar Petersen of Denmark, who had one of the best collections of accurately named old roses in Europe. This rose almost sneaks up on you. The flowers arrive in clusters of different pastel shades: yellow, pink, orange, salmon, and sometimes red. The blooms are small and lightly scented and are produced abundantly. The foliage is light green, and the growth is tall; the plant can be treated as a shrub or climber. It is sometimes reported to be the best rose in the garden. For something different, try this beauty.

GLAMIS CASTLE

Raised by *David Austin*
Parentage *'Graham Thomas' x 'Mary Rose'*
Introduced *1992*
Type *English Rose*
Size *1m*

Of all the white roses produced by David Austin, this would have to be one of the best. It has large to medium very double blooms on a sturdy compact plant, which grows to about 1m high. The flowering period has good continuity and the cup-shaped blooms are well scented with myrrh fragrance, and pure white when fully out.

GLOIRE DE DIJON

Raised by *Jacotot*
Parentage *'Desprez à Fleur Jaune' x 'Souvenir de la Malmaison'*
Introduced *1853*
Type *Noisette*
Size *4m or more*

The parentage is uncertain but that does not alter the beauty and the durability of this rose. In some places it has attracted almost saintly reverence. There is no doubt it is a treasure, having retained its popularity for 150 years. This is a happy rose in that it begins flowering early and tends to continue blooming right throughout the season. The blooms are about 10cm wide, quite double at times, quartered and buffy-orange in colour, sometimes deeper, sometimes lighter. The growth is fairly vigorous and the foliage is quite dense when the plant is young. It is significant that David Austin has frequently used this rose in his breeding programme.

GLOIRE DE FRANCE

Raiser and parentage *Unknown*
Introduced *1819*
Type *Gallica*
Size *1.5m*

In times gone by this was one of the popular Gallicas. The cupped and quartered blooms are rich pink overlaid with lilac tones and have a green eye when fully open. The fragrant flowers are freely produced.

1
GOLDEN CELEBRATION

Raised by David Austin
Parentage 'Charles Austin' x 'Abraham Darby'
Introduced 1992
Type English Rose
Size 2m x 2m

One of the largest of the English Roses, and at the same time one of the best. It has magnificently formed cupped, double flowers of a lovely shade of bronzy-gold. A very strong scent pervades the whole area where it is growing. The plant tends to spread, helped by the weight of the blooms, and it would not be difficult to make this excellent rose climb. In fact, it would not be difficult to imagine this rose 5m or more up a trellis.

2
GOLDEN WINGS

Raised by Shepherd
Parentage 'Soeur Thérése' x (R. altaica
x 'Ormiston Roy')
Introduced 1956
Type Shrub-climber
Size 3m

'Golden Wings' is a good example of a rose that exists only in shrub form but has the hidden talent to climb if encouraged to do so. There are examples of this rose being trained to climb to at least 5m. Once again we see toughness coming forward from one side of the parents. The large nearly 15cm flowers are just a little more than single and are lightly scented. They also have a large boss of golden stamens. The plant is wide growing with light green foliage, and flowers very well from mid-season to late. It is an excellent variety for many purposes but does need plenty of space.

GRAHAM THOMAS

Raised by David Austin
Parentage 'Charles Austin' x ('Iceberg'
x English Rose)
Introduced 1983
Type English Rose
Size 2–3m

Once in a lifetime a hybridist creates a rose of this calibre. The colour is superb, a deep buttery-yellow on opening, paling a little with age. The buds are fat and the flower opens cupped at first and flat across the top. The blooms are large and quite double with a muddled centre. The petals reflex a little with age. The flowers are borne singly, mostly in clusters, and a strong Tea Rose scent pervades the whole plant. We know of one plant that had 400 flowers on it at one time, and another that reached 5m high on the wall of a house. The growth is upright and vigorous with light green healthy foliage. This is a truly magnificent rose in every way and in 100 years time it may be said that this was the best of the Austin roses.

GREAT MAIDEN'S BLUSH

Raiser and parentage Unknown
Introduced Before 1738
Type Alba
Size 2m

When the genuine old roses are discussed it is not long before this beautiful old-timer enters into the conversation. It has two forms; the one illustrated has larger flowers, about 10cm wide, and the smaller form has flowers about 6cm across. They are otherwise similar except for the size of the plant. The flowers are pink to blush-pink, cupped and reasonably double with a pleasing fragrance. Like all members of this group, the plants are very hardy. One of the attractions of this rose is the way in which the lovely pink blooms are set off against the grey-green foliage.

GREENSLEEVES

Raised by Harkness
Parentage 'Rudolph Timm' x 'Arthur Bell'
Introduced 1980
Type Floribunda
Size 1m

My interest in old roses has always been apparent but alongside this, running parallel, was always an interest in roses that were different. 'Greensleeves' is certainly very different, and I saw it first in the Harkness glasshouses in 1984. It would be the best green rose available today. The pink buds open to flat chartreuse-green flowers, medium-sized and with no scent. When cut in the late bud stage they will open perfectly, while left on the plant they will discolour.

GROUSE-IMMENSEE

Raised by Kordes
Parentage 'The Fairy' x R. wichuraiana seedling
Introduced 1983
Type Rambler
Size 5m

I am never likely to forget this rose, as it is associated with one of the most embarrassing moments of my life. We were visiting Germany in 1984 and had arrived in Dortmund to visit Westfalen Park. We made our way successfully to the park and spent a wonderful day amongst a very large collection of roses, when a call of nature prompted me to find the nearest restrooms. Without much observation and being tired I entered one of the clearly marked rooms, only to be told very smartly to get out of the Ladies Room. Right at the door of the rooms was a large plant of 'Immensee' in full flower. This variety is a powerful grower and has single flowers about 6cm across, pink at first, fading to white. The flowering is prodigious and this rose has become important because of its relationship in the 'Flower Carpet' series.

GRUSS AN AACHEN

Raised by Geduldig
Parentage 'Frau Karl Druschki' x 'Franz Deegen'
Introduced 1909
Type Shrub
Size 1m

This rose arrived on the scene probably before its time. The Floribunda class was not known. It was different from Teas and Hybrid Teas, and for many years stood alone, much loved but isolated. When the Floribundas finally arrived, after World War II, it had something in common with them, but it was not until the English Roses made their appearance that it at last found some cousins and a family to belong to. It is a beautiful little rose. The blooms open blush-pink and fade to creamy-white, sometimes with the barest trace of pale pink. They are lightly scented, about 8cm wide and appear from summer to autumn.

ROSES HAVE
THORNS,
AND SILVER
FOUNTAINS MUD,

CLOUDS AND
ECLIPSES STAIN
BOTH MOON
AND SUN,

AND LOATHSOME
CANKER LIVES IN
SWEETEST BUD,

ALL MEN MAKE
FAULTS

WILLIAM SHAKESPEARE, 1564–1616

HAMBURGER PHOENIX

Raised by *Kordes*
Parentage *R. kordesii x seedling*
Introduced *1954*
Type *Shrub-climber*
Size *Over 4m*

The semi-double, large (10cm) flowers of this variety open wide and appear in small clusters on long, strong branches. The colour is bright scarlet and the blooms are lightly fragrant. This plant makes an excellent free-standing shrub or a low climber, depending on the way it is trained. It was introduced into New Zealand many years ago but the gardeners of the day were not ready for it. Now, with a new-found love for older-type roses, it is gaining popularity. Ever blooming, it makes a great splash of colour.

HANSA

Raised by *Schaum & Van Tol*
Parentage *R. rugosa hybrid*
Introduced *1905*
Type *Rugosa*
Size *1.5m*

Another beautiful variety of hybrid Rugosa, well worth a place in any garden. It has large flowers, deliciously fragrant, which are deep carmine-purple. They appear continuously over summer and autumn. Some may wonder why the word 'variety' is used in preference to the hybrid word 'cultivar'. I simply will not accept the use of any hybrid words or mispronunciation of others.

HAPPY CHILD

Raised by *David Austin*
Parentage *'Iceberg' x 'Hero'*
Introduced *1993*
Type *English Rose*
Size *1m*

An absolutely delightful rose that is a very useful addition to the yellows in the English Roses and also a fine example of a small-growing rose ideal for small gardens. The flowers are fully double and medium to large, cupped, quartered, and a glorious shade of deepest yellow. It has a delicious Tea Rose fragrance.

HARISON'S YELLOW

Raised by Harison
Parentage Chance seedling
Introduced 1830
Type Species Hybrid
Size 2m

This is the kind of rose that arouses the collector's interest. It is said that it was found as a chance seedling in a New York bank manager's garden. Great was the excitement when it became known that a double yellow rose was at last available. It is also said that it spread like a beautiful rash across the Eastern states of America, to be spread across the nation when the wagon trains set out for the goldfields of the West, leaving plants growing everywhere. It is reputed to be the 'Yellow Rose of Texas' and has also been called 'Ole Yella'. The mature plant is quite majestic at 2m, covered in summer only with medium double, golden-yellow blooms, sitting well in the ferny foliage. It is very hardy.

HEBES LIP

Raised by Paul
Parentage Damask x R. eglanteria
Introduced 1912
Type Damask Hybrid
Size 1m

This hybrid Damask is quite beautiful and distinct. The semi-double blooms are about 10cm across when open, and come from quite reddish buds, which open pure white with reddish-scarlet markings on the tips of the petals. In the middle is a group of bright gold stamens, which contrast beautifully with the rest of the flowers. There is a lovely Damask fragrance and the plant is compact.

HELEN KNIGHT

Raised by *Knight*
Parentage *R. ecae x R. spinosissima*
Introduced *1970*
Type *Species Hybrid*
Size *2m*

A comparative newcomer that has many attributes of roses of a much greater age. The 5cm-wide flowers are single with just five petals, deep golden-yellow in colour and spread profusely all the way along the arching branches. A beautiful sight in full bloom.

HENRI MARTIN

Raised by *Laffay*
Parentage *Unknown*
Introduced *1863*
Type *Moss*
Size *2m*

'Henri Martin' is probably the nearest to real crimson in the whole of the Moss family. One could not be blamed for thinking this rose is more modern than its introduction date. The flowers are nicely rounded, reasonably double and of a medium size. They open an intense crimson and, a day or two later, fade to deep, rich rosy-pink. The blooms are so consistently produced that at times the rounded plant could be mistaken for a camellia. The buds are lightly mossed and the blooms are quite fragrant.

1
HERITAGE

Raised by *David Austin*
Parentage *Unnamed seedling*
x ('Wife of Bath' x 'Iceberg')
Introduced *1984*
Type *English Rose*
Size *2m*

'Heritage' is one of the earliest of David Austin's introductions and one of the very best. This beautiful variety is as near to a classic old rose as you could get. The rounded blooms are cupped and flat across the open flower. The petals are nicely quartered, and the colour is blush-pink. The plant growth is strong with wiry stems and few thorns. The foliage is deep green and healthy. Under certain circumstances, that is, heat and humidity, rust can be a problem in New Zealand, but modern fungicides solve the problem quite easily.

2
HERMOSA

Raised by *Marcheseau*
Parentage *Obscure*
Introduced *1840*
Type *China Hybrid*
Size *1m*

This delightful, tidy little plant always seems to be in flower. It is thought that there is some Bourbon, as well as China, in this rose. It is certainly a little beauty with smallish pink and lilac blooms that are produced prolifically. They are cupped and have a light scent. There is also a climbing form of this rose called 'Setina', which is very beautiful in its own right, with arching branches covered with blooms.

3
HONORINE DE BRABANT

Raiser and parentage *Unknown*
Introduced *Prior to 1850*
Type *Bourbon*
Size *2m*

A grand old favourite from the early part of the nineteenth century, this rose has had varying periods of popularity. Of all the striped roses known, this variety would probably be the least conspicuous of all. The base colour is lilac-pink overlaid with a crimson and purple mottling. Light green foliage supports a vigorous plant and it can be made to climb. It is well scented.

4
HUGH DICKSON

Raised by *Dickson*
Parentage *'Lord Bacon' x 'Gruss an Teplitz'*
Introduced *1905*
Type *Hybrid Perpetual*
Size *Up to 2m*

Nearly a hundred years after its introduction, this rose still commands attention. Not only have many of the old roses survived but, with man's assistance in repropagating, their beauty of form has been preserved for us to enjoy and admire today. The very large double flowers are freely produced on a tall-growing plant. They are a deep rich crimson with a lovely scent.

IPSILANTE

Raiser and parentage Unknown
Introduced 1821
Type Gallica
Size 1.5m

This beautiful member of the Gallica family has huge flowers of bright cerise-pink. It is quartered, nicely fragrant and summer-flowering only. It was probably named after a Greek national hero. Well worth growing.

IRISH FIREFLAME

Raised by Dickson
Parentage Unknown
Introduced 1914
Type Hybrid Tea
Size 2m

Some years ago, while travelling through the suburbs of the city of Christchurch on a balmy summer's evening, we noticed a fine flowering shrub, absolutely covered in flowers. On closer examination we found it to be a very large plant of 'Irish Fireflame' smothered in blooms. It was at least 2m high and almost as wide, standing in the grounds of an almost derelict house. The blooms of this variety are large, about 13–14cm, single and very fragrant, with long reddish-pink buds opening to an exquisite flower of orange to old-gold shades.

ISPAHAN

Raiser and parentage Unknown
Introduced Before 1832
Type Damask
Size 1.5m

When we think of the Damasks as a whole, our thoughts perhaps roam to the creation of rose waters and some of the tales from the Middle East that have been handed down to us. If you had room in your garden for one Damask only, then perhaps this rose would be your choice. It is one of the first Damasks to open and one of the last to finish flowering – the period of bloom can extend over six to eight weeks. Sumptuous flowers of a beautiful medium-pink quite literally cover the large plant, and are strongly fragrant. From a distance this magnificent plant could be mistaken for a camellia in full bloom.

JACQUENETTA

Raised by *David Austin*
Parentage *Unknown*
Introduced *Unknown*
Type *English Rose*
Size *1.5m*

This rose has now been discarded by the house of Austin but that is no reason why we cannot grow and enjoy this very beautiful variety. Yes, in hindsight it does not conform to the criteria of an English Rose, but then if this view were generally held, many roses would have been lost. The flowers of 'Jacquenetta' are large, up to 12cm, semi-double, pale apricot in the bud opening to a paler apricot-blush. Many people have come to love its simple charm and it is nicely fragrant.

JACQUES CARTIER

Raised by *Robert*
Parentage *Unknown*
Introduced *1868*
Type *Portland*
Size *1.5m*

The Portland group came from diverse backgrounds and, because of circumstances at the time, they did not last long in popularity. 'Jacques Cartier' is a fine example of the type. A distinctive feature of the Portlands is the way in which the flowers are supported by quite short stems, sitting rather neatly in the foliage. The blooms are medium sized, very double, and quartered with a button eye. They are light pink, deeper in the middle, and very fragrant.

JAMES MITCHELL

Raised by *Verdier*
Parentage *Unknown*
Introduced *1861*
Type *Moss*
Size *2m*

This is one of the first Mosses to flower. When it reaches the peak of its blooming season the lovely, large rounded plant is covered with many perfectly shaped flowers. The dainty well-shaped buds are mossed brown-green and develop into bright cerise-pink blooms that pale to pinkish-lilac. They are medium sized, 6–8cm, opening flat with a button eye.

Some years ago, in the middle of a beautifully fine South Canterbury day, we had just completed lunch and I was returning to my particular task and necessarily had to pass the Damask group. My fantail pigeons were housed in several dove-cotes nearby and one particular male bird was always picking on the other birds, especially the females. In passing, this particular male bird was annoying the others and I called out, 'Leave her alone you silly old b.....' Almost immediately a man's voice answered, 'I never touched her.' It turned out that a couple had parked their car out on the highway and had been enjoying their walk around the garden unobserved, when my remark to the pigeon brought them out from the tall Damask family.

OVER!
THE SWEET
SUMMER CLOSES,
AND NEVER
A FLOWER AT THE
CLOSE,
OVER AND GONE
WITH THE ROSES,
AND WINTER AGAIN
AND THE SNOWS

ALFRED LORD TENNYSON, 1809–1892

JAYNE AUSTIN

Raised by *David Austin*
Parentage *'Graham Thomas' x 'Tamora'*
Introduced *1990*
Type *English Rose*
Size *2m*

'Jayne Austin' is one of the best to come off the English Rose production line. As with most establishments engaged in improving their product, this rose signals just that. It has a strong Tea Rose fragrance, and once it breaks into flower it has the breeding to repeat almost continuously. Looking at a picture of this rose it is easy to imagine that it is one of the classic old roses, except for its colour – apricot-yellow becoming apricot in the centre and paling towards the edges. The blooms are medium sized, about 8cm wide, cupped and flat. The petals have a silky sheen and the plant is healthy with deep green leaves. The colour of the blooms is very popular today.

JEAN DUCHER

Raised by *Ducher*
Parentage *Unknown*
Introduced *1873*
Type *Tea Rose*
Size *1.5m*

It is perhaps strange that this beautiful Tea Rose does not appear to have surfaced in the United Kingdom or Europe and yet it has been recognised in New Zealand for almost 100 years. It grows over 1m high and just as wide. The foliage is leathery and healthy and the flowers are large and a little more than semi-double. The buds are at first globular, opening wide and ageing from a soft salmon and lemon to a peachy shade. They are pleasantly fragrant with a Tea scent. As this is a Tea Rose it may not be very hardy in a cold climate. This is a beautiful rose that comes from a gentler time.

JOHN CLARE

Raised by *David Austin*
Parentage *'Wife of Bath'*
x 'Giant Meyer'
Introduced *1994*
Type *English Rose*
Size *1.5m*

Now and again a rose comes forward that has a display of colour and happiness that exceeds other attributes usually looked for in roses generally. 'John Clare' has medium-sized, cupped, light crimson flowers produced continually from spring to autumn. It has a light fragrance.

opposite →

JOSEPH'S COAT

Raised by *Armstrong & Swim*
Parentage *'Buccaneer' x 'Circus'*
Introduced *1964*
Type *Shrub-climber*
Size *2m*

An attractive semi-double rose that is known for its subtle changes of colour. Gold, yellow, red, orange, pink and crimson all feature in these colour changes. As with all roses of this type, take off or shorten side growth to make it grow tall, or trim back the tall shoots to make it shrub-like.

JUDE THE OBSCURE

Raised by *David Austin*
Parentage *'Abraham Darby' x 'Windrush'*
Introduced *1995*
Type *English Rose*
Size *2m*

Apart from anything else, David Austin will be remembered for the totally different roses he created. This rose is no exception. It has large incurved blooms, opening enough to reveal the yellow to lemon colour inside and the soft yellow outside. In fact you could call it honey-coloured. The blooms are cupped and have an unusual strong fragrance.

KATHARINA ZEIMET

Raised by Lambert
Parentage 'Étoile de Mai' x 'Marie Pavié'
Introduced 1901
Type Polyantha
Size 1m

Now and again a rose shows its pretty little face when many people have thought it lost. This little gem surfaced in East Germany in 1988 at Sangerhausen. Since its arrival in New Zealand it has become very popular. Of compact growth, it will reach a rounded plant of about 1m. The attractive mid-green shiny foliage and wiry growth supports a charming display of near pure white rosettes, which at first can be quite greenish. The small blooms are packed on a large head and have a pleasant light scent.

KATHRYN MORLEY

Raised by David Austin
Parentage 'Mary Rose' x 'Chaucer'
Introduced 1990
Type English Rose
Size 1.5m

Clear pink flowers, paler at the edges, sit upright on a healthy plant. This is one of the best English Roses and inevitably it will be popular. The flowers are fragrant, large and many-petalled, and repeat very well throughout the season. It is named after Mr and Mrs Eric Morley's daughter who passed away at only seventeen years of age. The Variety Club of Great Britain auctioned the name in aid of the Shaftesbury Homes. It raised £13,000.

FAR-OFF,
MOST SECRET AND
INVIOLATE ROSE,

ENFOLD ME
IN MY HOUR OF
HOURS

W. B. YEATS, 1865–1939

KEW RAMBLER

Raised *At Kew*
Parentage *R. soulieana*
x 'Hiawatha'
Introduced *1913*
Type *Rambler*
Size *Up to 5m*

KIFTSGATE

Raised by *Murrell*
Parentage *R. filipes x seedling*
Introduced *1954*
Type *Species Hybrid*
Size *10m or more*

KÖNIGIN VON DÄNEMARK

Raised by *Booth*
Parentage *R. alba*
x R. damascena
Introduced *1826*
Type *Alba*
Size *1.5m*

Another rose with greyish-green foliage, which obviously comes from *R. soulieana*. The flowers are single, bright pink towards the edge, and white in the centre. The blooms are 4cm across, very fragrant, and appear in prolific clusters all over the plant. It is summer-flowering only and has its peak on or about the longest day. Different, beautiful, fragrant and vigorous – what more is needed?

One of the most powerful-growing roses in commerce today. It could easily reach 10–15m up a tree, and has reached exactly that at the home of the Royal National Rose Society in England. The 3–4cm single flowers develop into huge rounded heads of about 100 flowers, which are followed by tiny crimson fruit. The whole mass develops the most powerful perfume and everything looks well in the greyish-green foliage.

Summer-flowering only, this rose has quite fragrant, quartered double flowers of a bright deep pink at first but fading slowly to medium pink and finishing pale pink. Grey-green foliage on a sturdy plant compliments the beautiful blooms.

LADY HILLINGDON

Raised by *Lowe & Shawyer*
Parentage *'Papa Gontier'
x 'Mme Hoste'*
Introduced *1910*
Type *Tea Rose*
Size *1.5m*

Colour is very difficult to repeat in roses. Even with the many thousands of roses that have been introduced in the last 200 years it is unlikely that any two of them are really alike. Probably that is one of the main reasons why they are so hard to identify. 'Lady Hillingdon' blooms are long, pointed and, when open, an attractive shade of warm apricot with a strong Tea fragrance. The growth is wiry and tough, reminding the viewer of one of its parents, 'Papa Gontier'. Perhaps the flowers tend to hang down a little when they are fully open, but this was true of many of the early Teas. There is also a very fine climbing sport of this rose. In our town there used to be a beautiful specimen, which reached all of 6m wide and over 2m tall and literally covered its netting support. This wonder to behold was a traffic-stopper, but beauty was not in the eye of the recent owner and it is now gone.

LADY PENZANCE

Raised by *Lord Penzance*
Parentage *R. eglanteria x R. foetida bicolor*
Introduced *1894*
Type *Species Hybrid*
Size *2m*

In the 1890s Lord Penzance was responsible for creating a group of roses that became known as the Penzance Hybrids. In light of the many roses that have been introduced since those times, this group was perhaps never exciting, but still has a place in history. This particular variety is one that always excited some comment. The flowers are single and smallish, of orange and lemon colour, and are sparsely set among the 'Eglanteria'-type foliage, which is strongly green apple scented. Is this where the green apple fragrance comes from for modern shampoo?

LA FRANCE

Raised by *Guillot Fils*
Parentage *'Mme Victor Verdier'
x 'Mme Bravy'*
Introduced *1867*
Type *Hybrid Tea*
Size *1m*

It is always possible to express doubt about the authenticity of the names of roses. In fact this seems to happen quite frequently. This rose has had some doubt expressed about it, but we must retain the present name until such time as proper credentials are produced. 'La France' is nevertheless a very important rose. Reputed to be the first Hybrid Tea after the long reign of the Hybrid Perpetuals, it was in fact many years before its time. A high, pointed bud develops into a magnificent flower of pink and silver that is nicely fragrant. Although not so eye-catching today, it remains historically important.

LAMARQUE

Raised by *Maréchal*
Parentage *'Blush Noisette'*
x 'Parks' Yellow Tea Scented China'
Introduced *1830*
Type *Noisette*
Size *Up to 5m*

It has often been said that you can measure the hardiness or otherwise of your climate by whether this rose will grow well for you. We are fortunate that it does very well for us, although we keep it as a large shrub rather than growing it as a climber. Probably the best-known plant of 'Lamarque' I know is in the garden of the late Nancy Steen in Remuera, Auckland. It grows on a boundary fence and is suspended into a nearby tree at a suitable height to walk under so that the blossoms can be seen to advantage. The large, loose blooms are pure white with pale lemon-yellow in the middle. They are very fragrant and quite double and usually appear in groups of three to five.

LA VILLE DE BRUXELLES

Raised by *Vibert*
Parentage *Unknown*
Introduced *1849*
Type *Damask*
Size *1.5m*

LAVENDER LASSIE

Raised by *Kordes*
Parentage *Unknown*
Introduced *1959*
Type *Shrub-climber*
Size *3m*

Occasionally this rose is described as a Hybrid Musk, but it seems to fit more easily with the classification given above. It is a vigorous grower – sometimes the long shoots reach at least 4m. It can easily be grown as a climber or a shrub. The colour is difficult to describe and under my local conditions does not see much of the lavender mentioned in its name. It may be that in another place at another time it can be quite lavender. At best it is pink with the lightest of mauve shadings. The flowers are of medium size and fragrant. They are quite double and plentiful, and the plant flowers repeatedly. This is an excellent choice if you are looking for something a little different to vary your planting scheme.

When thinking of the beautiful Damask roses, this one must be high up on the favourite list. Everything about it is large but not excessive. The plant grows vigorously with large, light green leaves, and the blooms are large, very double and very fragrant. They are an even rich pink all over with no fading, at least in the early stages of development, and later they reflex towards the outer edge and show a button eye. This is a sumptuous flower in every way.

opposite →

L. D. BRAITHWAITE

Raised by *David Austin*
Parentage *'Mary Rose'*
x 'The Squire'
Introduced *1988*
Type *English Rose*
Size *1.5m*

What at first sight appeared to David Austin a very beautiful rose, with hindsight and the passage of time he is now able to discard some varieties from his list, although their spirit lives on in later members of the family. In this case 'The Squire', a lovely rose in its own right, has passed on its spirit to 'L. D. Braithwaite'. Massive flowers developing from fat buds make this spreading plant very impressive to see for the first time. It is a lovely shade of even, deep scarlet-crimson, and the flowers are cupped and quartered. The fragrance appears to become stronger as the flower ages. A magnificent variety that produces majestic blooms.

LEANDER

Raised by *David Austin*
Parentage *'Charles Austin'*
seedling
Introduced *1982*
Type *English Rose*
Size *2m*

It would be true to say that when a rose is introduced it sometimes does not live up to expectation. On the other hand, sometimes a rose comes before the public with lesser publicity, and with the passage of time turns out to be a very good variety that becomes extremely popular. 'Leander' is such a rose, and it appears to improve with time. It is a tall grower and can be trained as a climber or a shrub. The blooms are medium sized, about 8cm wide, and appear in clusters. The colour is basically apricot but with shades of pink, cream and salmon. The flowers open out to a neat rosette.

LÉDA

Raiser and parentage *Unknown*
Introduced *Prior to 1827*
Type *Damask*
Size *1.5m*

This is a rounded, compact plant with strong, healthy foliage. The buds are reddish-brown and almost always appear to have been chewed by something. However, they eventually end up as a very double, pure white flower with a neat button eye and rolled centre. The reddish colour from the buds appears on the edge of the petals of the blooms, in what could be called a picotee effect, which gives credence to its common name of 'Painted Damask', as if the edges of the white petals have been brushed with red. The blooms are nicely scented.

LÉONTINE GERVAIS

Raised by *Barbier*
Parentage *R. wichuraiana*
x 'Souvenir de Catherine Guillot'
Introduced *1903*
Type *Rambler*
Size *5m or more*

'Léontine Gervais' is a vigorous rambler with slender stems and branches, and long wiry growths with shiny foliage and deep bronze young shoots. It is an attractive plant even without flowers. The blooms are sweetly scented, medium sized, cupped at first and opening to semi-double, palish salmon-orange flowers ageing to a creamy yellow. They arrive in clusters and make a fine display in mid-summer with some intermittent flowers later.

LEVERKUSEN

Raised by *Kordes*
Parentage *R. kordesii*
x 'Golden Glow'
Introduced *1954*
Type *Shrub-climber*
Size *4m*

This very beautiful rose is little known to many people. It has that basic strength and toughness of many roses created by the German rose growers of Kordes, who are now into their fourth generation of hybridists. Other rose breeders have also used it as a parent. The plant is vigorous with bright green serrated foliage and arching branches. The blooms are medium sized, 10cm across, semi-double, and a lovely shade of lemon-yellow, with exposed stamens. It has a nice scent.

LITTLE WHITE PET

Raised by *Henderson*
Parentage *Sport from 'Félicité et Perpétue'*
Introduced *1879*
Type *Shrub*
Size *Up to 1m*

There will always be some doubt about the origin of this rose but it remains after all this time an important small white rose, excellent as a bush or short standard. The small, very double flowers are many petalled and form a lovely rosette. The blooms come from fat red buds and appear all over a compact tidy plant. They have a light fragrance.

At the time of the commencement of our rose collection more than thirty years ago, there would have been perhaps only fifteen or twenty different ramblers available in New Zealand. By building up contacts in numerous countries over a long period of time, we were able to import into New Zealand at least 150 varieties of ramblers, most of which had never been seen here before, and some of which would correct the misnaming of several that had entered into the realms of confusion. It may be that New Zealand does not require so many varieties of ramblers, but the fact remains that they exist and should be recorded in book form so that their beauty will not be lost forever.

LOUISE ODIER

Raised by *Margottin*
Parentage *Unknown*
Introduced *1851*
Type *Bourbon*
Size *2m*

Although the Bourbon family came from quite mixed parentage, they were for many years some of the most beautiful of the classic old roses. They had the form of being very double, very fragrant, and of course they could flower on into the autumn. Now, with the advent of David Austin's English Roses, the Bourbons have competition for their position in the rose world. 'Louise Odier' is a most beautiful shade of bright rose-pink with a trace of mauve, very double, cupped, quartered and nicely fragrant.

← *opposite*

LOUIS XIV

Raised by *Guillot Fils*
Parentage *Unknown*
Introduced *1859*
Type *China*
Size *1m*

After many years of importing, there will always be some varieties that stand out. The experience is much like that of a hybridist, who waits more than patiently for his seedlings to flower for the first time. Likewise, when you import old varieties that you have not seen before, the expectation is great and almost cannot be contained. This rose in particular was a joy to see for the first time and, after more than thirty years, it is still exciting. The small, black, fat buds open to medium-sized semi-double blooms of rare beauty and fragrance. They remain quite blackish-crimson and the variety is equally useful as a compact bush or small-growing standard.

1
MADAME ALFRED CARRIÈRE

Raised by *Schwartz*
Parentage *Unknown*
Introduced *1879*
Type *Noisette*
Size *5m*

There seems to be some doubt about the exact classification of this rose, but it is most often placed in the Noisette group. It is possible that if we did discover the parents, we might be very surprised. It is my feeling that we do not usually see this rose at its best in New Zealand. At Mottisfont Abbey, in the south of England, there is an extremely fine specimen growing against a brick wall. It is at least 5m wide and more than 3m tall. During mid-summer it is a sight to behold, with its large, fragrant, double white blooms with just a touch of cream.

2
MADAME ALICE GARNIER

Raised by *Fauque*
Parentage *R. wichuraiana x 'Mme Charles'*
Introduced *1910*
Type *Rambler*
Size *5m*

'Mme Alice Garnier' is very sweetly scented with small, very double, quilled blooms of medium to soft pink, sometimes with apricot in the middle. The foliage is dark, glossy, abundant and healthy, with bronze young shoots. In some ways this rose could be likened to a fatter 'Cécile Brünner', but at other times, especially when open, it does not resemble it at all. This important acquisition to the Rambler group will thrive in most positions and can be used for extensive groundcover work, for covering walls, banks, fences, pillars and tank-stands, and also makes an excellent weeping standard.

3
MADAME HARDY

Raised by *Hardy*
Parentage *Unknown*
Introduced *1832*
Type *Damask*
Size *1.5m*

This superlative rose has been written about many times. The purest of white flowers develop from plump, creamy-white or blush-pink buds. They are lemon scented, medium sized, cupped, very double, and quartered with a green button eye. It has been said that this is the most exquisite rose of all and that as one of the classic old roses, few others can come near it for sheer perfection. Praise indeed, but then again, it deserves it.

4
MADAME JULES THIBAUD

Raised by *Unknown*
Parentage *'Cécile Brünner' sport*
Introduced *Unknown*
Type *Polyantha*
Size *1m*

Many people thought that this rose was lost, but it came to light in Otago, New Zealand, some years ago. It forms the fourth of the group that includes 'Cécile Brünner', 'Perle D'or', 'White Cécile Brünner' and 'Madame Jules Thibaud'. In fact, there is a fifth member called 'Pasadena Tournament', also known as 'Red Cécile Brünner'. 'Madame Jules Thibaud' has foliage and growth similar to the others, but the flowers have more petals and there are times when they are quite deep pink, especially when newly opened. Sometimes there is a little orange in the throat, which pales with age. Because of the manner of the new season's growth (like the others in the group) it is difficult to obtain sufficient budwood to create enough plants to meet the ever-present demand.

On my travels throughout the countryside of Britain, I was very impressed with and envious of the use of bricks everywhere. It seems they are very compatible with roses, being used for pathways, driveways, walls of all heights, archways, towers, pillars and all manner of buildings, as well as steps and stairways in all shapes and sizes. Probably it is the lovely natural earthy colour of brick that fits it so well with roses. The brick walls used as shelter and support adjacent to many important rose gardens are magnificent structures. It is likely that most of them were built many years ago when labour and materials were relatively inexpensive. It is important to remember the tremendous influence these walls and other structures have had on roses. First, they provide almost maximum shelter for plants. A young rose planted at the base of a wall in the case of a climber or rambler, or nearby in the case of a bush or shrub, would have immediate protection from icy blasts, which can be so damaging to young soft growth. These walls give a measure of secure support, which other types of material and shelter fences can never give. Once a climbing or rambling rose is established on such a solid structure it is there for a lifetime, with the possible exception of broken ties. These majestic constructions, reaching at times 3–4m high, also always retain a measure of warmth even on their exposed side, which is of paramount importance when establishing young roses in a colder climate, and when these walls are used to surround gardens their beneficial effect is increased many times.

MAGENTA

Raised by Kordes
Parentage 'Lavender
Pinocchio' x seedling
Introduced 1954
Type Shrub
Size 1.5m

Although this rose is a reasonably recent introduction, it gains a place in this volume because of its old form. The growth is compact and, as for most of the shrub roses, about as wide as it is tall. The medium-sized blooms of 8cm are freely produced from early summer onwards, and are at first a lovely shade of deepish lilac-mauve, paling a little with age. They have a good scent and are quite double, appearing on arching branches in lovely sprays that are useful in floral arrangements.

MAGNIFICA

Raised by Dingee & Conrad
Parentage R. rugosa
x 'Victor Hugo'
Introduced 1909
Type Hybrid Rugosa
Size 1.5m

This rose is well named for it is truly magnificent when it is in full flower. The large 12–14cm blooms are the most beautiful shade of purple and are double and very fragrant. The plant has handsome green foliage. As a whole the Rugosas have had rather a raw deal from some rose enthusiasts. It seems to be a matter of acceptance. It was perhaps difficult for some to become used to the idea that these roses actually do perform as beautifully as other types. In fact most have several additional attributes. First, they can support attractive, fat, orange fruit while the plant is still in flower; secondly, almost all of the group grow excellently near the sea; and lastly, they are probably the hardiest of all the families.

MAIDEN'S BLUSH

Raiser and parentage Unknown
Introduced Before 1738
Type Alba
Size 2m

One of the beautiful and ancient members of the Alba family. If the stories are true that the Romans brought Alba roses to England, then this rose could have had very old parents, and it was probably present during some very important parts of history. Grey-green foliage is a feature of this healthy plant, which has large, double, cupped blooms of blush-pink that are nicely fragrant.

MAIGOLD

Raised by *Kordes*
Parentage *'Poulsen's Pink' x 'Frühlingstag'*
Introduced *1953*
Type *Shrub-climber*
Size *3m*

Once again we have a beautiful product from Kordes, who have the uncanny knack of introducing very fine roses with great regularity. The truth is probably that having existed through more than four generations, they have created a base from which they are able to be very selective in those they release. Some years ago, Wilhelm Kordes IV told me that they can grow 200,000 seedlings to select only two for one year's introductions. 'Maigold', by nature of its many prickles and distinctive foliage, shows its relationship to *R. spinosissima* through 'Frühlingstag', but do not let this discourage you from growing it. The flowers are large, double, very fragrant, and a lovely shade of orange-apricot. It has one massive summer flowering with some blooms later in the season.

MARÉCHAL NIEL

Raised by *Pradel*
Parentage *Seedling of 'Isabella Gray'*
Introduced *1864*
Type *Noisette*
Size *Up to 5m*

This is another representative of the beautiful Noisette family that is distinctive in its own right. Like many of them, it requires some shelter from the coldest of temperatures. The flowers open from long, pointed, yellow buds to butter-yellow blooms of great beauty and fragrance. Because the flowers are heavy for the stalk immediately behind the flower, they always want to hang down, but if grown up a wall or into a tree, you will be able to look up into the colours of another era. There is a long established plant of 'Maréchal Niel' near York, in England, reputed to be 18m long by 3m tall.

MARIE PAVIÉ

Raised by *Alégatière*
Parentage *Unknown*
Introduced *1888*
Type *Polyantha*
Size *1m*

Old Polyantha roses appear from time to time and I was delighted to find this one in Sangerhausen. It is a sturdy, compact plant covered in masses of small (about · 3–4cm) rosette-type flowers. The foliage is large and bronzy and seems to be impervious to disease. The buds are fat and arrive in clusters, bursting into the prettiest blush-pink blooms of a rosette nature. They are deeper at first, paling later, and they have a lingering fragrance. This specimen is very useful for tubs and small gardens.

MARY ROSE

Raised by *David Austin*
Parentage *'Wife of Bath' x 'The Miller'*
Introduced *1983*
Type *English Rose*
Size *1.5m*

When David Austin introduced 'Constance Spry' and 'Chianti' in 1961 and 1967 respectively, it could be said that the English Roses had arrived, even though neither of these would flower again in a season. It now seems incredible that another two English Roses, 'Mary Rose' and 'Graham Thomas', should be introduced at the Chelsea Flower Show, side by side, in 1983. If not before, the English Roses had now definitely arrived. It is also remarkable that after eighteen years in commerce these two are still two of the most popular-selling roses around the world. There is no doubt that 'Mary Rose' brought the Damask roses into the twentieth century. To all intents and purposes, this lovely hybrid is an ever-blooming Damask, which under favourable climatic conditions can literally be in flower continuously. It is a large, rounded shrub with medium to large blooms of bright pink that have a lovely fragrance. This rose was named after Henry VIII's flagship, which was recovered from the Solent after more than 400 years at the bottom of the sea.

MAXIMA

Raised by Unknown
Parentage Possibly related to 'Maiden's Blush'
Introduced Unknown but very ancient
Type Alba
Size 2m

The large flowers of this splendid, classic old rose are creamy-white with muddled centres and are quite fragrant. They are sparingly arranged on a tall plant among the lush grey-green foliage. It has been said that this was the rose used as an emblem by Bonnie Prince Charlie and his followers. One has to ask whether a rose that flowers for about two months of the year would have been useful in this way. It is tough and will grow well in the coldest climates.

MAY QUEEN

Raised by Manda
Parentage R. wichuraiana
x 'Champion of the World'
Introduced 1898
Type Rambler
Size 5m

Another rambling rose of distinction with very healthy foliage and unusual-looking flowers that are medium-sized and light pink on the outside and a deeper cerise-pink in the centre. They are quite double and the petals appear to be crinkled in an attractive way. A tough, healthy rose useful for all purposes.

MEG

Raised by *Gossett*
Parentage *'Paul's Lemon Pillar'*
x 'Madame Butterfly'
Introduced *1954*
Type *Climber*
Size *4m*

Long slender buds produce large 12cm blooms with about ten petals showing red stamens. They are pinkish-apricot with a nice fragrance and have the ability to flower well early, with some good flowers later. The large blooms do change into large fruit, which can be left if desired or removed. A very fine rose.

MERMAID

Raised by *Paul*
Parentage *R. bracteata*
x unknown Tea Rose
Introduced *1918*
Type *Climber*
Size *Up to 10m*

This rose is either loved or hated, probably brought about by whether you have planted it in the right or the wrong place. 'Mermaid' is an exceedingly strong grower, and although it may be slow to develop, it does grow in massive manner in later life. Therefore, if you plant it with plenty of room for it to develop, you will love it, and if you have a cramped position you will more than likely end up cursing it. The flowers are large, all of 12–15cm, with just five petals. When fully open they expose stamens of a bronze colouring that remain part of the plant's display even after the petals fall. The blooms are golden-yellow and have a strong fragrance. The growth is very vigorous and the stems are well covered with large hooked thorns.

OH, NO MAN KNOWS THROUGH WHAT WILD CENTURIES ROVES BACK THE ROSE

WALTER DE LA MARE, 1873–1956

MISTRESS QUICKLY

Raised by David Austin
Parentage 'Blush Noisette'
x 'Martin Frobisher'
Introduced 1995
Type English Rose
Size 1m

Here we have an unusual rose in that it is hardly an English Rose, coming from the above parents, but this does not prevent it from being a lovely rose in its own right. The flowers are small, about 5–6cm across, plentifully produced, and are rich pink at first, fading to lighter pink. Because of its disease-free outlook on life it makes an excellent subject for small gardens and borders. It is almost continually in flower.

←— *opposite*

149

MOLINEUX

Raised by *David Austin*
Parentage *'Golden Showers' seedling x seedling*
Introduced *1994*
Type *English Rose*
Size *1m*

Up to the present, this would have to be the deepest golden-yellow rose David Austin has produced. At the same time, it would be one of the most compact growers in the English Rose group. The colour is almost indescribable, being a very deep golden-yellow tinted with deep orange at times. The flowers are medium-large, quartered, open very flat, and have a strong Tea Musk fragrance. It is excellent for bedding or border planting. Entering the realms of impossibility, I would like to see the faces of the French rose growers of 200 years ago if they could see this variety. They would not believe their eyes.

MOONBEAM

Raised by *David Austin*
Parentage *Unknown*
Introduced *1983*
Type *English Rose*
Size *2m*

In the early days of hybridising at David Austin Roses, quite a number of roses were created and introduced that, with the passage of time, have now been superseded or simply dropped because they do not now fit the more strict criteria being applied. 'Moonbeam' is one of these roses. It has tall, upright growth, freely producing large semi-double flowers. They are about 14cm wide and just a little more than single. The creamy, long, pointed buds, with the barest flush of apricot, open to a lovely flower with a delicate scent. 'Moonbeam' is definitely a collector's item.

MOONLIGHT

Raised by *Pemberton*
Parentage *'Trier' x 'Sulphurea'*
Introduced *1913*
Type *Hybrid Musk*
Size *2m*

This is another of the Rev. Joseph Pemberton's beauties, with Peter Lambert's 'Trier' lurking in the background. 'Moonlight' has small to medium flowers, semi-double, opening wide in clusters. They are yellowish in the bud and open to creamy-white with prominent golden-yellow stamens. The blooms are striking against the glossy, dark bronzy foliage. The other parent of 'Moonlight' was 'Sulphurea', a yellow Hybrid Tea introduced by W. Paul in 1900.

MOYESII GERANIUM

Raised by *Mulligan*
Parentage *R. moyesii Hybrid*
Introduced *1938*
Type *Species Hybrid*
Size *2.5m*

Whenever a rose is sought after for hips or fruit in the autumn, inevitably the *R. moyesii* group come into the discussion. You may have read that 'Geranium' is the shortest among them, but remember that this means at least 2m. It is unquestionably a most beautiful and interesting rose. The medium-sized single blooms are a most intense orange-scarlet. They have attractive stamens that are very prominent. When the blooms pass, the fruit develops into long (8–9cm) flagon-shaped beauties. They are at first lime-green in late summer and, as the weather cools, they turn fiery orange and make a magnificent sight.

MRS OAKLEY FISHER

Raised by *Cant*
Parentage *Unknown*
Introduced *1921*
Type *Hybrid Tea*
Size *1m*

This is one of the treasures that have survived from the 1920s. It is a beautiful, small-growing rose with single, five-petalled blooms about 8cm across. They are a most unusual colour of buffy-apricot with prominent stamens. The growth is thin and wiry and looks as if it would not support a tough compact plant. It will flower from early summer until the end of autumn.

MUTABILIS

Raiser and parentage *Unknown*
Introduced *Unknown but*
very old
Type *China*
Size *3–5m*

There is no possible way that the age of this rose will be known. It could have existed in China for centuries or it could be a rose created by an astute Chinese gardener who had been growing roses from seed. In any event, it is a truly interesting and fascinating rose. With the arrival of 'Masquerade' on the scene, the rose world became excited because it was thought that the first rose to deepen in colour had arrived, but in fact 'Mutabilis' pre-dated it by a long time. This unusual rose is as good as single and about 7–8cm wide, with a group of small stamens. The colour changes commence with buds that are orangish-yellow opening to an almost coppery-yellow, then changing to coral-pink and finishing a darkish burned purplish-crimson.

THIS LITTLE
FLOWER THAT LOVES
THE LEA,

MAY WELL MY SIMPLE
EMBLEM BE;

IT DRINKS HEAVEN'S
DEW AS BLITHE
THE ROSE,

THAT IN THE KING'S
OWN GARDEN
GROWS

SIR WALTER SCOTT. 1771–1832

NEW DAWN

Raised by *Somerset Roses*
Parentage *Sport of 'Dr W. Van Fleet'*
Introduced *1930*
Type *Climber*
Size *5m*

In every group or sub-group of the rose family there are several varieties that stand out from the rest. They do so because they are happy roses. These are the ones that thrive in most places without any problems. 'New Dawn' is a happy rose and not only has it become very popular around the world, but it has passed its genes onto many other varieties. The sweetly scented flowers are medium to large with pink shading when open, paling to blush-pink with age. They are lightly double and open wide showing golden stamens. The growth is almost rambling with long wispy branches that can be easily trained. Altogether an excellent rose.

NOBLE ANTONY

Raised by *David Austin*
Parentage *('Lilian Austin' x 'The Squire')*
x ('Fragrant Cloud' x 'Glastonbury')
Introduced *1995*
Type *English Rose*
Size *1.1m*

Beautifully fragrant, this introduction from David Austin is one of those varieties that is difficult to describe when it comes to colour. It lies in the territory between a deep pink and a light red. I will dodge the issue and describe it as cerise-crimson. It is double with many petals, and flowers plentifully on a compact tidy plant, useful for bedding or borders.

← *previous page*

NOZOMI

Raised by *Onodera*
Parentage *'Fairy Princess' x 'Sweet Fairy'*
Introduced *1968*
Type *Procumbent*
Size *3m*

I had the pleasure of seeing the original plant of 'Nozomi' in the garden of Toru Onodera at his home in the suburbs of Tokyo. It was a splendid sight, the plant being absolutely saturated with small, single, shell-pink blooms. Little did Toru Onodera know that he had created a rose that would be quickly accepted and used by other hybridists worldwide. He has also introduced three other roses of the same type but different colours. These are 'Suma', 'Akashi', and 'Miyagino'. 'Nozomi' was the name of Toru Onodera's niece, who died when she was very young.

NUITS DE YOUNG

Raised by *Laffay*
Parentage *Unknown*
Introduced *1845*
Type *Moss*
Size *1m*

'Nuits de Young' is well known for the fact that it is the darkest of the Moss roses. It is also known in some quarters as 'Old Black'. It grows into a tidy, compact plant, which during the summer season sports a lovely display of small to medium double blooms of the deepest crimson-maroon and rich purple with a few yellow stamens.

OFFICINALIS

Raiser, parentage and introduction *Unknown*
Type *Gallica*
Size *1m*

Steeped in history, this rose has had many stories told about it. One that can be believed comes from one of its popular names, the 'Apothecary Rose'. It is now well recorded that early armies were accompanied by herbalists and others who treated the soldiers with healing balms, ointments, potions, baths, etc, using materials based on the products from roses. The flowers of this particular rose are bright scarlet, up to 12cm across, a little more than single, open out quite flat with stamens showing, and are very fragrant. It is generally accepted that this was also the 'Red Rose of Lancaster'.

OLD BLUSH

Raiser and parentage *Unknown*
Introduction date *Unknown but of great antiquity*
Type *China*
Size *1.5m*

It is interesting that two very old roses should follow each other. Although they come from two different continents and each in its own way is so diverse, they have much in common. As with the former, this rose has a number of alternative names, indicating that at different periods of time, in different countries, this rose was known and loved. It was introduced into Europe about 1750, but there is no doubt that it was known in China for a very long time. It was part of the gene pool that came to the Western world from the Far East and in a peaceful revolution changed the summer-flowering only roses into all-season blooming roses. The rose-pink, loosely double flowers of 'Old Blush' are medium sized and appear from early summer through to winter. There is a climbing form of this fine old variety, which can easily reach up to 15m.

EACH MORN
A THOUSAND
ROSES BRINGS,
YOU SAY;
YES,
BUT WHERE
LEAVES THE
ROSE OF
YESTERDAY?

THE RUBÁIYÁT OF OMAR KHAYYÁM

OLD DANISH

This rose is a mystery to me in every way, hence no picture, but it does serve to prove two points – one about the naming of a rose, and the other, how they can sometimes be distributed unknowingly, adding to the ever-mounting confusion already discussed about the correct naming of roses. Many years ago, as was our policy to re-import varieties that perhaps needed to be re-identified or had developed some health problem, a request was made to Valdemar Petersen of Denmark to send in our consignment of budwood some wood of 'Dorothy Perkins', a rambling rose of some popularity and which seemed to us to be not the correct one. The parcel duly arrived, passed through the usual channels, and finally I took the bucket containing twenty-five varieties of old roses in budwood form down to the nursery and budded them onto suitable stocks in our quarantine area. At this time I placed ten buds from two sticks of budwood, five from each stick, of 'Dorothy Perkins' onto the rootstocks. When the buds began to grow there was obviously some difference in the two groups of five. Even when they were only 3cm high they were different. As the plants grew, they developed very differently from each other. I wrote to Denmark to try to get the situation clarified, and the next year I actually visited Petersen's nursery but could not find the strange variety anywhere. I carried out all the research I possibly could but to no avail. In desperation I finally called this rogue rose 'Old Danish'. It was a lovely rose, far too refined to be discarded. It is an attractive, free-growing climber with handsome foliage, and medium-sized, cupped, double blooms of a lovely shade of lilac-pink. It is probably a climbing Bourbon, and is delightfully fragrant. Recently a lady asked me, 'Do you know a rose called "Old Danish"?' She had tried to find it listed but was not successful. I answered, rather sheepishly, 'Yes.'

OMAR KHAYYÁM

Raised by *Unknown*
Parentage *From seed from Omar Khayyám's grave*
Introduced *1893*
Type *Damask*
Size *1m*

This rose has very double pink flowers, nicely fragrant, and of small to medium size with what could be described as quilled petals. The growth is thick, the plant compact, and the branches very prickly. A really different and interesting rose.

ORANGE TRIUMPH

Raised by *Kordes*
Parentage *'Eva' x 'Solarium'*
Introduced *1937*
Type *Hybrid Polyantha*
Size *1m*

At the time of the introduction of this rose, it excited great comments from the gardeners of the day. The Polyantha family, which had held sway between the two World Wars, suddenly had a rose that was a colour break and very healthy and durable. It gained in popularity until the advent of the Floribundas. Growing about 1m high, it was used for bedding all over the world. The flowers are quite small, about 3–4cm, appear in upright clusters, and are a medium red with a light scent. The name causes some confusion in that it was called 'Orange Triumph' after the House of Orange in Holland, rather than for its colour.

HOW FAIR IS THE ROSE!
WHAT A BEAUTIFUL FLOWER,
THE GLORY OF APRIL
AND MAY!

BUT THE LEAVES ARE
BEGINNING TO FADE
IN AN HOUR

AND THEY WITHER AND
DIE IN A DAY.

YET THE ROSE HAS ONE
POWERFUL VIRTUE
TO BOAST,

ABOVE ALL THE FLOWERS
OF THE FIELD;

WHEN ITS LEAVES ARE ALL
DEAD, AND FINE COLOURS
ARE LOST,

STILL HOW SWEET A PERFUME
IT WILL YIELD!

ISAAC WATTS, 1674–1748

PARKDIREKTOR RIGGERS

Raised by *Kordes*
Parentage *R. kordesii*
x 'Our Princess'
Introduced *1957*
Type *Shrub-climber*
Size *4m*

This rose has the inbuilt ability to perform well and is another excellent crimson rose from the House of Kordes. Its flowers are deep, velvety crimson, a little more than single, and of medium size, about 8cm. They open out flat and the petals are wavy. As many as forty to fifty blooms can appear on one large head. The flowering period extends from early summer to late autumn. This attractive rose makes a magnificent addition to any garden.

PAT AUSTIN

Raised by *David Austin*
Parentage *'Graham Thomas'*
x 'Abraham Darby'
Introduced *1995*
Type *English Rose*
Size *3m*

This is a rose that caused quite a bit of consternation in the Austin household because it was felt it did not conform to the accepted pattern of an English Rose. However, in the end it was introduced and has already made its mark within the family. The deeply cupped flowers are large with bronzy-orange colour on the inside of the petals and a light coppery-yellow on the outside. They are sweetly fragrant and reasonably double.

← *opposite*

PAUL TRANSON

Raised by *Barbier*
Parentage *R. wichuraiana*
x 'L'Ideal'
Introduced *1900*
Type *Rambler*
Size *5m or more*

In every country I have visited, 'Paul Transon' has been present, and this has to be the hallmark of this excellent Rambler from Barbier. This is a happy rose that does well in most situations. It can be a rampant grower with long arching branches. The foliage is dark and glossy and the young growth bronzy and dark, which makes a lovely setting for the medium-sized 8–10cm sweetly fragrant blooms. The flowers are a little unusual in that the petals appear quilled. The colour is a rich salmon-pink at first, deeper in the centre, paling towards the edges later. This is a beautiful, useful and attractive variety that could find a place in every garden.

PEGASUS

Raised by *David Austin*
Parentage *'Graham Thomas'*
x 'Pascali'
Introduced *1995*
Type *English Rose*
Size *2m*

A new variety from David Austin with many fine attributes. The spreading habit of the plant lends itself to being trained as a climber if required, while the healthy foliage seems disease free. The large double flowers of about 10–12cm open wide and flat; the colour being a rich buffy apricot-yellow towards the centre, paling to cream towards the edges. It has a rich Tea Rose fragrance and is not unlike 'Buff Beauty' in looks and habit.

PENELOPE

Raised by *Pemberton*
Parentage *'Ophelia' x 'William*
Allen Richardson' or 'Trier'
Introduced *1924*
Type *Hybrid Musk*
Size *2m*

Despite the parents given for this fine rose, I can see no 'William Allen Richardson' in it at all. 'Trier' is nearer the mark as on a closer examination it is not unlike 'Penelope'. With hindsight, 'Penelope' helped to found the Pemberton dynasty of Hybrid Musks. The 'man of the cloth' became the 'man of the roses'. 'Penelope' has medium-sized, semi-double blooms that open pale pink but soon pass to creamy-white when fully open and flat. They are fragrant and the display of blooms looks very attractive on a healthy plant and last from early summer to autumn.

PERDITA

Raised by *David Austin*
Parentage *'The Friar'*
x (unnamed seedling x 'Iceberg')
Introduced *1983*
Type *English Rose*
Size *1.5m*

This was one of what David Austin regards as his first flush of English Roses to appear on the scene before the introduction of 'Graham Thomas' and 'Mary Rose' in 1986, which marked a new development in the English Rose. The blooms are large and many-petalled and have a strong fragrance. They are apricot in the bud and open paler to a cupped flower with an old look about them. The scent must be very good because 'Perdita' was awarded the Henry Edland Medal for fragrance in 1984. This is a healthy plant with a spreading habit of growth.

PERLE D'OR

Raised by *Rambaud*
Parentage *Polyantha*
x 'Mme Falcot'
Introduced *1884*
Type *Polyantha*
Size *1m*

'Perle d'Or' is another member of the 'Cécile Brünner' group, which has delighted gardeners for many years. One has to wonder why the many excellent hybridists worldwide have not created more of this particular type. 'Perle d'Or' is apricot-yellow in the bud, opening to yellow and paling towards the edges. Like its counterparts, the buds and flowers are exact miniatures of their larger relations. In every other respect it is typical of the group and has a lovely scent.

PHYLLIS BIDE

Raised by *Bide*
Parentage *'Perle d'Or'*
x 'Gloire de Dijon'
Introduced *1923*
Type *Rambler*
Size *5m or more*

It seems prophetic that the very next rose should have 'Perle d'Or' as one of its parents. 'Phyllis Bide' is one of the nicest happenings in the rose kingdom. It is a 'happy rose' and has the ability to flower for a very long time, even into the middle of winter in sheltered places. An individual bloom would never set the world on fire, but collectively a large spray is extremely beautiful. The flower is small, about 3cm, but when grouped, especially with the changes of colour from lemon-yellow in the bud to pink, from pink to rosy-pink, paling to shades of apricot and cream, it becomes a fine sight indeed. An extremely beautiful variety.

PINKIE

Raised by *Swim*
Parentage *'China Doll'*
open pollinated
Introduced *1947*
Type *Climbing Polyantha*
Size *3m*

Like its parent, this rose has a great abundance of bloom, making it very showy. The colour is the brightest pink with a faint trace of cerise in the mix. The flowers are 7–8cm wide, loosely semi-double and have a light scent. The climbing variety of 'Pinkie' perhaps is more attractive because of the great density of flowers on a much larger plant. If you like the colour it is worth a place in your garden.

PORTLAND ROSE

Raiser and parentage *Unknown*
Introduced *Prior to 1800*
Type *Portland*
Size *1m*

Shrouded in the mists of time we are left to deduce the origins of this rose and the rest of the group. The China Roses brought the recurrent gene to Europe and the Portland group was the first to be developed with their influence. They formed a bridge between the classical old roses with the once-flowering summer-only habit, and what was yet to come. However, while the Portland Roses were soon passed over, there were some very beautiful members of the group. This rose could be likened to the 'Red Rose of Lancaster' except that it has seasonal flowerings. It has large, semi-double, scarlet blooms with yellow stamens and quite a strong Damask scent.

PORTMEIRION

Raised by *David Austin*
Parentage *Unknown as yet*
Introduced *1999*
Type *English Rose*
Size *1.5m*

The medium to large-sized blooms are cupped and quartered and have a strong old rose fragrance. The colour is rich deep pink, similar to two other English Roses, 'Gertrude Jekyll' and 'John Clare', and like the latter variety has a prolific display of flowers. This rose is named for the Portmeirion Potteries Ltd from the city of Portmeirion in Wales.

POULSEN'S CRIMSON

Raised by *Poulsen*
Parentage *'Orange Triumph' x ('Johanniszauber' x 'Betty Uprichard')*
Introduced *1950*
Type *Hybrid Polyantha*
Size *1.5m*

If you admire this rose you may, as I do, ask why hybridists continue chasing the elusive dream when they already have in their hands the most wonderful creations. Often their efforts result in roses that are very near existing ones. You may also ask how such a beautiful crimson rose comes from the above parents, but when we realise that the 'Johanniszauber' part of the equation has 'Château de Clos Vougeot' blood in its veins, then all is clear. The beautiful crimson, almost single blooms are 5cm wide with a light scent and appear in large clusters.

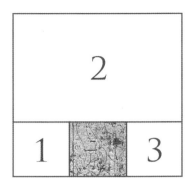

1
PRAIRIE HARVEST

Raised by *Buck*
Parentage *'Carefree Beauty'*
x 'Sunsprite'
Introduced *1985*
Type *Shrub*
Size *2m*

Because of my association with Roses of Yesterday and Today of Watsonville, California, I was privileged to receive many of Griffith Buck's roses from Iowa State University. He carried out a breeding programme to create varieties hardy enough for the tough climate of Iowa. We introduced up to thirty varieties created by Griffith Buck, and 'Prairie Harvest' has been one of the popular ones. The plant has an upright growth habit with light green, healthy foliage while the flowers are double, pointed in the bud, of pale lemon-yellow opening to nicely fragrant blooms of medium yellow.

2
PRÉSIDENT DE SÈZE

Raiser and parentage *Unknown*
Introduced *Prior to 1836*
Type *Gallica*
Size *1m*

This is one of the very old Gallicas, which could have been one of the thousands of field-grown seedlings that were hurriedly removed from the destructive path of the armies involved in the Napoleonic Wars. It is one of the most beautiful of the family. The unopened buds are pink, while the open flower is deep carmine-crimson at first, then paling to mauvish-white at the edges. It is nicely fragrant.

3
PRETTY JESSICA

Raised by *David Austin*
Parentage *'Wife of Bath'*
x seedling
Introduced *1983*
Type *English Rose*
Size *1m*

'Pretty Jessica' is a beautiful, small-growing rose that could be placed in any small garden. It has the look of a Centifolia, the strong old rose fragrance of yesteryear, and bright, rich pink double blooms for most of the season. What more could one ask? The growth of the plant is upright and the foliage reasonably healthy. The name, too, has a bearing on the popularity of this rose. It is amazing how many people have a Jessica in their family.

← *Portmeirion*

1
PROSPERITY

Raised by *Pemberton*
Parentage *'Marie Jeanne' x 'Perle des Jardins'*
Introduced *1939*
Type *Hybrid Musk*
Size *2m*

It is not impossible, as with most of this family, to train this rose as a climber. It has dark bronzy foliage and double medium-sized blooms, which appear on the plant in plentiful clusters. One of its parents, 'Marie Jeanne', was also a fine Hybrid Musk rose but its flowers were smaller.

2
QUATRE SAISONS

Raiser, parentage and introduction *Unknown*
Type *Damask*
Size *2m*

This rose also rejoices under the names of 'Autumn Damask' and 'Damascena Bifera'. There is little doubt that it has played an important part in the development of later varieties. Also known as the 'Rose of Paestum' and 'Pompeii Rose'; these names show its great antiquity and we are fortunate that it remains for us to admire. Its flowers are clear pink and richly fragrant, on a loose-growing shrub reaching about 2m. It is sought after because of its long flowering season right through to winter.

3
QUATRE SAISONS
BLANC MOUSSEUX

Raiser and parentage *Unknown*
Introduced *Before 1835*
Type *Moss*
Size *2m*

This rose is historically important and perhaps not so important as it might be. The buds are heavily mossed and they open out to white semi-double flowers with the gold stamens showing. Sometimes partly pink flowers appear or even completely pink flowers, showing its origins from 'Quatre Saisons'.

4
QUEEN NEFERTITI

Raised by *David Austin*
Parentage *'Lilian Austin' x 'Tamora'*
Introduced *1988*
Type *English Rose*
Size *1m*

A variable variety that can be beautiful or ordinary depending on the season. It has double yellow blooms freely produced over a tidy plant. It is named after one of the ancient queens of Egypt.

1	2
3	4

RADIO TIMES

Size *1m*

Raised by *David Austin*
Parentage *Unknown*
Introduced *1994*
Type *English Rose*

This rose has a lovely flower of clear rich pink, nicely double, of true rosette form, and quartered with a green eye. The fragrance is strong and the growth is compact and inclined to be spreading. It reminds one of the old Gallica shape.

← *opposite*

RAMBLING RECTOR

Raiser and parentage *Unknown*
Introduced *1912*
Type *Rambler*
Size *5m*

RAMONA

Raised by *Dietrich & Turner*
Parentage *Anemone sport*
Introduced *1913*
Type *Climber*
Size *3m*

In this so-called 'politically correct' world we live in today, one has to wonder whether it would be permissible to give a rose this title. However, this variety has been with us for a long time and in its own right is quite attractive. It is believed that it is probably a hybrid from *R. multiflora* and it does have some similarities. It has one long flowering season in mid-summer and the flowers are white, about 3cm wide, and semi-double with golden stamens. It is very durable and very vigorous.

An unusual climbing rose that needs shelter, not being particularly hardy, but if you have a position that suits it, it can be very beautiful. It has large, single, clematis-like flowers, carmine-pink in colour with stamens showing. The growth is sparse and the leaves rather like *R. laevigata,* from which it is suspected it comes. It is distinctive but beautiful.

RAUBRITTER

Raised by *Kordes*
Parentage *'Daisy Hill' x 'Solarium'*
Introduced *1936*
Type *Shrub*
Size *3m*

Although this rose can grow to 3m up a trellis or tripod, without that support it can be shaped into a 1m shrub, flowering only in the summer with a prolific display of small, cupped, bright pink blooms, which have the ability to hang down. There exists here the opportunity to use this rose as the basis for a group of truly cascading roses.

RED BLANKET

Raised by *Ilsink*
Parentage *'Yesterday' x seedling*
Introduced *1979*
Type *Procumbent Shrub*
Size *2m*

This rose sees another variation in the types of roses coming forward towards the end of the twentieth century. It seems that rose breeders in general are prepared to experiment more, with the final pressure going onto the survival of the Hybrid Tea class. 'Red Blanket' can be trained to climb, shaped to be procumbent, or shaped as a shrub. The semi-double flowers of about 6–8cm wide are deep reddish pink and quite attractive en masse. They pale towards the centre and have a good bunch of golden stamens.

REDOUTÉ

Raised by *David Austin*
Parentage *'Mary Rose' sport*
Introduced *1992*
Type *English Rose*
Size *1.5m*

Sometimes a rose breeder does not have to lift a finger to create a new variety, as in this case we have what is called a bud sport from 'Mary Rose'. To explain this happening, a rose plant growing happily in any situation has the ability to send up a branch with different-coloured flowers on it. Propagating material can be taken from this branch and budded onto rootstocks and, if the new variety proves stable, then production of it can be increased. 'Redouté' is in fact a pale pink form of 'Mary Rose' so it is exactly like its parent in every way except in colour.

RICHARDII

Raiser, parentage and introduction *Unknown*
Type *Species Hybrid*
Size *1m*

When the Aswan Dam project was mooted a long time ago and the intention to flood the Valley of the Kings was made known, it became necessary to relocate the temple of Abu Simbel and all of its treasure. In the process of accomplishing this aim, many very early artefacts were discovered including pollen grains and petals of a rose. It seems to be generally accepted now that these came from *R. richardii,* also known as *R. sancta,* 'The Holy Rose', and the 'Abyssinian Rose'. It has large single blooms, pointed buds in medium pink opening to blush-pink and white. The growth and foliage is very like a Gallica.

179

ROBIN HOOD

Raised by *Pemberton*
Parentage *Seedling x 'Miss Edith Cavell'*
Introduced *1927*
Type *Hybrid Musk*
Size *1.5m*

Usually placed in the Hybrid Musk group, this rose is so bright and so packed with flowers that it makes everything near it look sombre. This is not to say that 'Robin Hood' is not an attractive rose in its own right, but its brightness is perhaps not consistent with the more reserved shades of the genuine old roses. Its small, bright cherry-red blooms are so tightly packed on the plant at full flower that you cannot see much foliage at all. It is a tough shrub, suitable for many purposes.

ROGER LAMBELIN

Raised by *Schwartz*
Parentage *'Fisher Holmes' sport*
Introduced *1890*
Type *Hybrid Perpetual*
Size *1m*

The blooms of this variety are the deepest possible crimson with a thin white line around the petals of the open flower. It can have quite a striking effect on you when you see it for the first time. It is quite unusual and quite fragrant and reminds me of a Christmas cake decoration.

ROSA BANKSIAE LUTEA

Raiser and parentage
Unknown; native of China
Introduced *1824*
Type *Species*
Size *At least 5m*

The introduction date given here is misleading because this rose was probably known in China for thousands of years before it was taken to Europe. However, it is a much respected and desired member of the Species group. The plant is very vigorous in milder climates but can suffer frost damage in colder areas. Some retail outlets advertise it as hardy, which is not true and does mislead people. The flowers of this beautiful rose are tiny but prolific, appearing in clusters. The season extends for almost two months, from the moment the first tiny clusters break out on the sunny side of the plant until the last ones complete the display on the shady side. The branches are thornless and although it is said to be evergreen, this is true only in warmer climates. Any scent is difficult to detect.

ROSA BANKSIAE LUTESCENS

Raiser and parentage *Unknown*
Introduced *1870*
Type *Species*
Size *At least 5m*

There are four Banksia roses in cultivation: the double yellow, the single yellow, the double white and the single white. There are also two hybrids raised in Italy, both of which are now available. This rose, *R. banksiae lutescens*, has a lovely fragrance and is deep golden yellow in colour. It is a true single, having only five petals with prominent yellow stamens. The blooms appear in large clusters and are less than 3cm wide. The four introduced species of *R. banksiae* are similar in growth and foliage, with only minor differences in twigginess and colour of foliage.

ROSA BANKSIAE NORMALIS

Raiser and parentage
Unknown; native of China
Introduced *Before 1884*
Type *Species*
Size *At least 5m*

This is the form of *R. banksiae* that is naturalised in Western China. It is seen growing on the banks of streams and in gullies all over the area. We will never know, of course, if this was the original Species or not. It is strongly scented of violets, and the single white flowers of about 4cm wide are produced in clusters, which quite set the plant alight.

THIS IS THE WAY,
WALK YE IN IT.
THE WILDERNESS
AND THE
SOLITARY PLACE
SHALL BE GLAD
FOR THEM,
AND THE DESERT
SHALL REJOICE,
AND BLOSSOM AS
THE ROSE

← *Rosa Mundi*

ISAIAH 35:1

ROSA MUNDI

Parentage/origin *Colour sport from R. gallica officinalis*
Introduced *Prior to 1500*
Type *Gallica*
Size *1m*

Although the antiquity of this rose will always be disputed, it does not alter its unique beauty. It is one of the prettiest of all the old striped roses. Its botanical name is *R. gallica versicolor*, and it is part of the huge Gallica family. The flowers are basically pink with splashes of white and crimson and purplish-pink. There would be no two blooms exactly alike.

← *page 182*

ROSERAIE DE L'HAŸ

Raised by *Cochet-Cochet*
Parentage *Probably a sport from R. rugosa*
Introduced *1901*
Type *Hybrid Rugosa*
Size *1.5m*

'Roseraie de l'Haÿ' is a magnificent shrub rose with deep green foliage and evenly spaced blooms covering the nicely rounded plant. The flowers are a purplish-crimson and large, about 12–13cm wide. They are quite double and very fragrant but unlike most of the Rugosa group do not really set fruit.

ROSE-MARIE VIAUD

Raised by *Igoult*
Parentage *'Veilchenblau' seedling*
Introduced *1924*
Type *Rambler*
Size *4–5m*

Some pundits would have you believe that this seedling from 'Old Blue' is of no account but I can assure you it is a Rambler of some quality. The foliage and growth is very strong and the flowers open out in quite large clusters. Each tiny flower, about 3cm wide, is quite double and the colour range is quite amazing. There are shades of mauve, lilac, purple, grey, purplish-crimson and blush-mauve present in the cluster all at one time. There are five different purplish or mauve Ramblers and they are all useful in their own right.

ROSETTE DELIZY

Raised by *Nabonnand*
Parentage *'Général Galliéni'*
x 'Comtesse Bardi'
Introduced *1922*
Type *Tea Rose*
Size *2m*

A beautiful rose of varying colours, no doubt inherited from 'Général Galliéni', one of its parents. The blooms come from reddish buds, open to carmine-pink with lemon-yellow centres, then sometimes deepen to crimson-carmine as they age. Like all members of the Tea family it prefers a warmer situation.

ROTE MAX GRAF

Raised by *Kordes*
Parentage *R. kordesii seedling*
Introduced *1980*
Type *Procumbent Climber*
Size *4m*

This comparatively new procumbent rose has the most brilliant crimson-scarlet single flowers you could wish for. They have wavy petals and appear in clusters and are about 6–8cm wide, paling a little towards the centre. The plant develops long arching branches and when in full flower is a sight to behold. It has one long flowering season, lasting about two months and falling between those that flower early and again later. This rose can be trained to climb or ramble and could just as easily fall over a bank or terrace.

RUGSPIN

Raised by *Petersen*
Parentage *Rugosa seedling*
Introduced *Unknown*
Type *Hybrid Rugosa*
Size *1.5m*

For many years I was able to import beautiful old roses from my old friend Valdemar Petersen of Löve in Denmark. His roses were always accurately named and always arrived in excellent condition. He sometimes slipped one of his own creations into the parcel and this was how 'Rugspin' arrived in New Zealand. It is truly a beautiful rose. The blooms are 13–14cm wide and the five single petals are royal purple in colour followed by large, fat, orange fruit. It is a very fragrant rose that will remain a lasting memory to a fine, dedicated rosarian.

SAFRANO

Raised by *Beauregard*
Parentage *Unknown*
Introduced *1839*
Type *Tea Rose*
Size *1m*

As with all the old Tea Roses this variety requires a measure of shelter to get the best out of it. The blooms are pale apricot from long pointed buds opening to semi-double large flowers that have the usual delightful Tea scent. A gem from the past.

SAINT CECILIA

Raised by *David Austin*
Parentage *'Wife of Bath' x seedling*
Introduced *1987*
Type *English Rose*
Size *1.5m*

In the main, the naming of David Austin's English Roses has been original. Other rose breeders have in some cases resorted to using names that have already been used, and by doing this have added to the confusion. The cupped blooms are of medium size, nicely fragrant, and of a pale buffy-apricot, paling to blush-pink. This rose was named for the patron saint of musicians.

SAINT SWITHUN

Raised by *David Austin*
Parentage *'Mary Rose'*
x ('Chaucer' x 'Conrad
Ferdinand Meyer')
Introduced *1994*

Type *English Rose*
Size *2m*

Again an extremely beautiful rose with very large flowers of an exquisite soft pink fading to blush-pink. It has a powerful fragrance and the plant grows tall and can easily be made to climb.

following pages ⟶

SALLY HOLMES

Raised by *Holmes*
Parentage *'Ivory Fashion' x 'Ballerina'*
Introduced *1976*
Type *Hybrid Musk*
Size *2m*

Some people may raise their eyebrows at this rose being placed among the Hybrid Musks, but it has just as much right to be placed with them as anywhere else. The large single flowers appear in clusters and the plants are literally choked with blooms. Creamy-white at first, they become white and are fragrant. It has been said that there are too many blooms on the heads and this tends to make the branches blow around somewhat. No doubt this rose will be used for future breeding, as it seems to be strong in all facets of the hybridiser's requirements.

SANDERS' WHITE RAMBLER

Raised by *Sanders*
Parentage *Origin unknown*
Introduced *1912*
Type *Rambler*
Size *5m*

Over a long period of time a white Rambler with tight little rosette flowers has been grown in New Zealand. It was known as 'Sanders' White'. But after three journeys to the United Kingdom and Europe, I realised that the rose grown in these countries under that name was different. We now grow that rose and it has slightly bigger, pure white blooms that are not quite so double as the former one, and it is possible to see golden stamens in the centre. The new version is fragrant and has deep green glossy foliage that contrasts beautifully with the white flowers. It blooms from early summer through to autumn, performs well as a Rambler, and is excellent trained on a pole or grown as a weeping standard.

SARAH VAN FLEET

Raised by *Van Fleet*
Parentage *R. rugosa*
x 'Mt Maryland'
Introduced *1926*
Type *Hybrid Rugosa*
Size *2m*

This lovely hybrid has clear, rose-pink, semi-double blooms of medium size, which are cupped at first and open to show gold stamens. Among the attributes of the Rugosa roses and their hybrids are their resistance to disease and to wind, particularly salt-laden wind, and their ability to survive in cold climates.

opposite —→

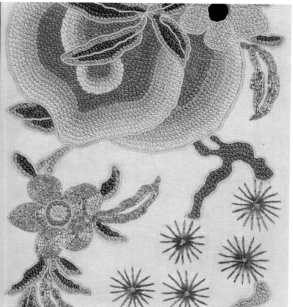

SCARLET FIRE

Raised by *Kordes*
Parentage *'Poinsettia' x 'Alika'*
Introduced *1952*
Type *Shrub*
Size *3m*

Always attractive, this rose makes a fine display with both flower and fruit. The German hybridising firm of Kordes has for decades had the ability to create absolutely beautiful and different roses, and this is another of them. The plant grows to more than 2m, and when in bloom can be totally covered in large, almost single, bright scarlet flowers, stamens showing, followed by a crop of large, fat, orange fruit.

SCEPTER'D ISLE

Raised by *David Austin*
Parentage *Unnamed seedling x 'Heritage'*
Introduced *1996*
Type *English Rose*
Size *1.5m*

This rose received the Edland Award, which is awarded each year by the Royal National Rose Society for the best scented rose. It has medium-sized flowers, which are cupped and reasonably double. The colour is a pleasant shade of softish lilac-pink. It would be excellent for planting in the border, the shrubbery or the rose garden.

opposite →

1
SCHNEEZWERG

Raised by *Lambert*
Parentage *R. rugosa x R. bracteata*
Introduced *1912*
Type *Hybrid Rugosa*
Size *1.5m*

Whether or not the parentage given above is correct does not alter the fact that this rose is unique. It has deep green, small foliage and the blooms are snow-white, medium-sized and semi-double. They open flat with quite prominent lemon-yellow stamens. After the flowers pass there is a good crop of small scarlet fruit. There are plenty of light green thorns.

2
SEA FOAM

Raised by *Schwartz*
Parentage *'White Dawn' x 'Pinocchio'*
Introduced *1964*
Type *Shrub-climber*
Size *3m*

The breeding given above is not accurate but it does involve the same parents at least three times. This rose seems to be in no man's land, between a shrub and a climber. It makes an excellent shrub that spreads and gains height with age, while if trained to climb it will do so, although it certainly takes time to achieve this object. However, it is an excellent rose – tough, wiry, procumbent if need be, prolific in flower and lightly scented. The blooms are 3–4cm wide, developing from fat pink buds, usually opening blush-pink and with a little age becoming creamy-white. They are quite double, rosette type, and packed tightly on the plant, blooming from summer to autumn.

3
SEAGULL

Raised by *Pritchard*
Parentage *R. multiflora seedling*
Introduced *1907*
Type *Rambler*
Size *6m or more*

'Seagull' is a very effective pure white rambling rose that has one summer flowering season each year. It is believed to be very near to *R. multiflora* but this variety has double white blooms in heavy clusters and they are very fragrant. They show the stamens in the centre and it would cover a large area when given the chance.

4
SEMI-PLENA

Raised by *Unknown*
Parentage *Sport of R. alba maxima*
Introduced *Ancient*
Type *Alba*
Size *2m*

Graham Thomas, the doyen of old roses, writes: 'The white roses (the Albas) are supreme over all the other old races in vigour, longevity, foliage, delicacy of colour, for they embrace some exquisite pink varieties, and purity of scent.' 'Semi-plena' is a fine tribute to an excellent group. Its toughness, durability and disease-resistance come from its relationship with *Rosa canina*. This rose is believed to be the 'White Rose of York'. It has grey-green healthy foliage, medium to large, almost single blooms with a good fragrance. It is one of several roses in the group from which Attar of Roses is distilled.

SEMPERFLORENS

Origin *Unknown*
Parentage *R. chinensis derivative*
Introduced *1792*
Type *China*
Size *Less than 1m*

This very bright crimson, small, cupped rose grows quietly in many gardens and I am sure the owners do not realise how important it has been. No one knows for how many centuries this and its near relatives 'Fabvier' and 'Cramoisi Supérieur' grew in Chinese gardens, but when it was introduced into England in the late eighteenth century, it brought about a peaceful revolution in roses in two ways. First, it brought its lovely colour, which really had not been seen in that part of the world before. Secondly, it introduced the recurrent gene into roses, which created many new groups within the genus. This historic rose deserves more recognition. It is also known as 'Slater's Crimson China'.

SHARIFA ASMA

Raised by *David Austin*
Parentage *'Mary Rose'*
x 'Admired Miranda'
Introduced *1989*
Type *English Rose*
Size *1.5m*

Probably in the top three English Roses for fragrance, this rose grows into a very sturdy plant with upright growth and solid leathery foliage. The flowers are medium to large and open to delightful blooms, which are very double, quartered at first and later open to a muddled centre. They are medium to light pink, paling towards the edges, and have a strong, delicious fragrance.

SIR EDWARD ELGAR

Raised by *David Austin*
Parentage *'Mary Rose'*
x 'The Squire'
Introduced *1994*
Type *English Rose*
Size *1.5m*

Again an excellent variety that has medium to large blooms that are many-petalled and lightly scented. The colour is in that range of – is it light red or is it deep pink? They definitely have some cerise or carmine in them and depending on the weather can be lighter or darker.

SISSINGHURST CASTLE

Origin, parentage and date of introduction *Unknown*
Type *Gallica*
Size *At least 1m*

When one thinks of the stories about the roses raised by the French growers in the early nineteenth century, and how many Gallicas were among them, it is amazing that so many of them have survived to this day; and it is even more amazing that accurate names have accompanied them. One of the roses is 'Sissinghurst Castle', the name given to it by Harold Nicholson and Vita Sackville-West, those consummate gardeners, when they discovered it in the grounds of their home in the 1940s. More recently it is thought to be 'Rose des Maures'. The plum-coloured, medium-sized flowers are fragrant and have muddled centres, showing some stamens.

SOMBREUIL

Raised by *Robert*
Parentage *'Gigantesque' seedling*
Introduced *1850*
Type *Climbing Tea Rose*
Size *At least 4m*

Often when customers ask for an old climbing rose it takes a little time to establish exactly what they are looking for, and after this has been done, more often than not this is the rose chosen – especially if it happens to be in flower at the time. It has a very good Tea scent and the open flower is large (10–12cm) and literally packed with petals that appear to be quilled at first and then become muddled. It opens very flat and is creamy-white. There always seems to be a flower on the plant, which has long branches, good foliage and large thorns. It is an excellent variety for every reason.

SOPHY'S ROSE

Raised by *David Austin*
Parentage *'Prospero' x unnamed seedling*
Introduced *1997*
Type *English Rose*
Size *1.5m*

The flowers of this variety open broad and rather flat and are attractively rosette shaped. They have a light Tea fragrance and are light crimson or quite deep pink. The plant is compact and healthy and quite literally covered with flowers, which perhaps look more like peonies than roses.

A ROSE IS
FAIREST WHEN IT'S
BUDDING NEW,

AND HOPE IS
BRIGHTEST WHEN IT
DAWNS FROM FEARS,

AND ROSE IS
SWEETEST WASHED
WITH MORNING DEW,

AND LOVE IS
LOVELIEST WHEN
EMBALMED IN TEARS

SIR WALTER SCOTT, 1771–1832   *Sir Edward Elgar* →

SOUVENIR DE LA MALMAISON

Raised by *Béluze*
Parentage *'Mme Desprez'*
x a Tea Rose
Introduced *1843*
Type *Bourbon*
Size *1m*

'Souvenir de la Malmaison' is probably the first old rose that comes into people's minds, even when they do not know its name. This wonderful variety conjures up the best features for those who are new to the older-type roses. It seems to have everything. The fragrant flowers are large – at least 12cm across – well filled with petals and nicely quartered. The colour is an attractive shade of pink across most of the bloom except near the edges, where it becomes creamy. The flower develops from a very fat, rounded bud and when open is flat across the top. A good climbing form is available and is very popular.

SPARRIESHOOP

Raised by *Kordes*
Parentage *'Baby Château'*
x 'Else Poulsen'
Introduced *1953*
Type *Shrub-climber*
Size *4m*

The House of Kordes in Holstein, Germany, must have thought a great deal of this rose to have named it after the district in which their nursery is situated. This is a hardy plant with strong, tall branches and large thorns. The blooms are 10cm across and have shades of pink, apricot and salmon, and are paler in the centre with a fine group of stamens. They are just a little more than single and nicely fragrant, and arrive in clusters. The healthy plant seems to be continuously in flower.

STANWELL PERPETUAL

Raised by *Lee*
Parentage *R. damascena semper-florens x R. spinosissima*
Introduced *1838*
Type *Species Hybrid*
Size *2m*

This rose originated as a chance seedling in a garden at Stanwell in Essex. In many well-established gardens, rose seedlings have a habit of popping up anywhere and most of them amount to nothing of importance, but sometimes one turns out to be a beauty. That is the case with this chance hybrid. It is a superlative rose in every way. When Mr Lee named it 'Perpetual' he recorded probably its finest feature. The large healthy plant with greyish fern-like foliage really is never without flower. They are of medium size, about 9cm wide, flat and double and a little deeper than blush-pink when opening, and paling later.

SUMA

Raised by *Onodera*
Parentage *Seedling of 'Nozomi'*
Introduced *1989*
Type *Procumbent Shrub*
Size *1m*

This is a lovely, small-flowered, procumbent variety that can be used as a groundcover or made to climb. It also does well as a short standard. Not unlike 'Nozomi' in its habit and foliage, the flowers are small, about 2cm across, quite double, and a nice purplish-red in colour.

SWEET JULIET

Raised by *David Austin*
Parentage *'Graham Thomas'*
x 'Admired Miranda'
Introduced *1989*
Type *English Rose*
Size *1.5m*

There is no doubt that when used as a parent, 'Graham Thomas' has a strong influence on its progeny. The plant growth and foliage of 'Sweet Juliet' have been influenced in this way. The upright, healthy growth supports ample blossoms of medium size. They are cup-shaped and of a pleasant buff-apricot and yellow colouring – shading that has become very popular in recent years – and they have a strong Tea scent.

SWEGINZOWII

Native of North West China
Introduced *1909*
Type *Species*
Size *3m*

Apart from *R. moyesii,* this would probably be the best Species for the most beautiful fruit. They come in groups of three to five and are about 8cm long, starting quite greenish-bronze in the autumn and then changing to fiery orange as the weather gets colder. The flowers are about 5cm across, single and light pink in colour. The foliage is fern-like.

201

As I approach the final parts of this volume, I believe some comments have to be made about the change David Austin has made to all families of roses. He has worked quietly on his projects and ambitions in the Shropshire countryside. We, that is the rose lovers of the world, are well aware of what was available family-wise before the Austin phenomenon, and we know of the great work done by rose hybridisers at all times and in all countries, and yet whether we are aware of it or not, David Austin has changed the rose world as never before. The results of his work have now superseded many of the varieties we knew of the old families. He has created roses that look like Gallicas, like Centifolias, like Hybrid Musks, like Damasks, like Bourbons, and many that look old but are distinctive in their own right. The difference in all these roses is that there is now a greater colour range available, and the flowering season has also been lengthened.

IF AUTHORS
WROTE OF ROSES
ALL THE
LIVELONG DAY,

AND PAINTED
THEM IN WORDS
TO MATCH THEIR
SWEETNESS,

THEY WOULD
NEVER TELL
ONE HALF OF THE
GLORY OF
THE QUEEN
OF FLOWERS

HELEN CROFTON

TEASING GEORGIA

Raised by David Austin
Parentage 'Charles Austin' x unnamed seedling
Introduced 1998
Type English Rose
Size 2m

Particularly nice cupped blooms of medium to large size (about 10–12cm wide) cover a strong-growing plant with a graceful habit of growth. The flowers are very double, quartered with a small green eye in the centre, and the colour is deep golden-yellow with a flush of orange when it is first out. It has a lovely Tea Rose fragrance.

← previous page

TESS OF THE D'URBERVILLES

Raised by David Austin
Parentage 'The Squire' x unnamed seedling
Introduced 1998
Type English Rose
Size 2m

David Austin has said that this red rose of his creation is probably the best all-round deep red rose he has bred. It has large double blooms with many petals, which are cupped with the petals reflexing with age. They are deep crimson with a strong fragrance. This fine variety is a robust plant with healthy growth and foliage.

opposite →

A rose grower, collector or rose enthusiast is not like other collectors who shut themselves up and lock away their treasures. On the contrary, he possesses such an abundance of prizes that he can afford to distribute much of his wealth. Svend Poulsen

THE DARK LADY

Raised by *David Austin*
Parentage *'Mary Rose' x 'Prospero'*
Introduced *1991*
Type *English Rose*
Size *1.5m*

Sometimes the choosing of a name does make it difficult later. In this case, 'The Dark Lady' refers to one of Shakespeare's characters and not to the fact that the flowers are a dark red. They are not, but they are a lovely shade of crimson with a shade of purple in them. They are nicely double, cupped at first and quite fragrant. The blooms look well against the dark green, healthy foliage.

THE FAIRY

Raised by *Bentall*
Parentage *'Lady Godiva' sport*
Introduced *1932*
Type *Polyantha*
Size *1m*

It is a little difficult to write about a rose that is so universally popular. No matter which country you visit, this rose has been accepted and used by all. It is found almost everywhere. The fact that it is so well used seems to ignore its inherent fault that it has no scent. However, it has many other good features. Probably its popularity comes first from its colour, and secondly from its hardiness and prolific flowering. The colour is bright clear pink and the blooms, although small, arrive in clusters, literally covering the plant in full bloom. It is extremely hardy and can be used for many purposes including tubs, standards and groundcover.

THE GARLAND

Raised by Wells
Parentage R. moschata x R. multiflora
Introduced 1835
Type Rambler
Size 3–4m

'The Garland' is a rampant, vigorous grower that has a superlative display in mid-summer only. The 3cm blooms are set out in clusters, and the individual flowers are not unlike a double daisy, billowing out from the centre exposing the stamens. The flowers appear in shades of lemon and pink, paling to white, and of course have a powerful fragrance.

THE PILGRIM

Raised by David Austin
Parentage 'Graham Thomas' x 'Yellow Button'
Introduced 1991
Type English Rose
Size 1.5m

This rose could very easily be taken for an old one. The only feature that gives it away is its lemon colour, a shade not present in the classic old roses. The flowers of this beautiful hybrid are large, up to 10–12cm wide, and, when open, very flat and packed with petals, a form not unlike the Tea Rose 'Sombreuil'. It has a strong fragrance and is bound to become popular. No doubt in the future its progeny will have a great influence in this changing world of rose form.

| 1 | 2 |
| 3 | 4 |

1
THE PRINCE

Raised by *David Austin*
Parentage *'Lilian Austin' x 'The Squire'*
Introduced *1990*
Type *English Rose*
Size *1m*

There is no doubt that this is a rose of superb colour. It is the deepest, richest crimson, which changes soon to a rich royal purple, reminiscent of the lovely dark shades of the Gallicas. The blooms can be affected by the hot summer sun but the early and late flowers can be quite magnificent. The dark foliage is a nice contrast to the lovely rosette shape of the dark flowers.

2
TOUR DE MALAKOFF

Raised by *Soupert & Notting*
Parentage *Unknown*
Introduced *1856*
Type *Centifolia*
Size *2m*

A very distinctive rose from yesteryear. The colours present in the flower at different times are purple, cerise, grey, mauve, lavender and magenta-pink. The blooms are loosely double and quite large, and the changing of the colours reminds me of my music teacher, who wore scarves or kerchiefs of these shades. The plant grows in a spreading manner and needs staking.

3
TRADESCANT

Raised by *David Austin*
Parentage *'Prospero' x ('Charles Austin'*
x 'Gloire de Dijon')
Introduced *1993*
Type *English Rose*
Size *1m*

Both the John Tradescants, father and son, would never have believed they would have a rose named after them. These inveterate plant collectors brought back many plants to England from their respective journeys to the Americas. Probably the smallest of the dark red English Roses, they purple with age.

4
TREVOR GRIFFITHS

Raised by *David Austin*
Parentage *'Wife of Bath' x 'Hero'*
Introduced *1994*
Type *English Rose*
Size *1.5m*

If the Tradescants would have been surprised had they known a rose was named after them, I can assure the reader that the name recipient of this rose was more than surprised. Having worked with and studied roses all my life it came as an unexpected honour. I will let David Austin describe it for you: 'Beautiful flowers, opening flat and dusky pink, against fine, dusky green foliage. The growth tends to be low, the branches growing outwards to make a shapely shrub. The leaves are of a dusky green, echoing the colour of the flowers to good effect. An attractive and rather different variety of truly old rose character. A beautiful old rose fragrance reminiscent of a fine oaky claret.'

TRICOLORE DE FLANDRE

Raised by *Van Houtte*
Parentage *Unknown*
Introduced *1846*
Type *Gallica*
Size *Over 1m*

Another of the very beautiful striped old roses, 'Tricolore de Flandre' is in some ways not unlike 'Camaieux', and is sometimes mistaken for it. This hybrid has a spreading growth habit, and the flowers are of medium size, double and nicely fragrant. The blooms would originally have been white with heavy striping of crimson-purple, purple, and lilac-mauve. Some rose enthusiasts have been known to look down on striped roses but they are beautiful and distinctive in their own right and make a marvellous contrast when planted among other colours.

TRIER

Raised by *Lambert*
Parentage *Probably 'Aglaia' seedling*
Introduced *1904*
Type *Hybrid Musk*
Size *4m*

Whether the above parentage is correct or not, one has to ask if Peter Lambert ever dreamed that this rose would become so important. It has semi-double, small, fragrant blooms in large clusters. They are lemon-blush at first, becoming blush-pink and white. The two major contributors to the creation and development of the Hybrid Musks were Peter Lambert and Joseph Pemberton, and both used 'Trier' in their respective work. Their resultant efforts speak for themselves, and again we have the example of a humble rose of no great expectation becoming the basis for the dedicated work of two men and the creation of a new rose type.

Trier is a beautiful city in south-eastern Germany, about fifteen kilometres from the Luxembourg border. It is a city steeped in history, having been founded by the Romans over 2000 years ago; in fact it had its 2000th anniversary in 1985 and Kordes named a rose 'Trier 2000' in its honour. Walking around the city, which is nestled in the bends and banks of the Moselle, a wine-growing area, one can see the remains of the black gate or Porta Nigra, one of the four gates of entry to the city; the amphitheatre, where no doubt the Romans had their own kind of sports; and the baths, where they had perfected a method of heating water. No one will ever accurately know what peoples passed through the valley, but Trier was a crossroads where armies and travellers frequently stopped. It is interesting to note that the Roman name for the city was 'Trevorum'.

TRIGINTIPETALA

Raiser and parentage *Unknown*
Introduced *Unknown, but very old*
Type *Damask*
Size *2m*

Correctly named *R. damascena trigintipetala,* this old variety became the basis of the distillation of Attar of Roses, used in the cosmetic and perfume industry. It is a very old industry and one that is still functioning in many countries such as France, Turkey, Egypt, India, Morocco, Spain, Bulgaria and Iran. Several years ago some 7500 acres of roses were grown in Bulgaria and the Kazanlik Valley for this purpose, and in recent years the production of Attar is known to have increased. In the old Soviet Union this rose was hybridised with several near relations in an attempt to improve the quality of Attar. This rose is a lusty, healthy grower and has medium-sized, medium-pink loose blooms with a typically strong Damask fragrance.

TUSCANY SUPERB

Raised by *Unknown*
Parentage *Possibly a 'Tuscany' seedling*
Introduced *Before 1848*
Type *Gallica*
Size *2m*

Whoever named this fine rose certainly knew what they were doing because it is superb. Few classic old roses command such immediate attention and complimentary remarks as this hybrid. A plant in full display covered in medium-sized crimson-purple double blooms is a joy to behold. When fully open a few stamens are visible and there is quite a strong fragrance. The petals are often used in the making of pot pourri.

MADE WEAK
BY TIME
AND FATE,
BUT STRONG
IN WILL TO
STRIVE,
TO SEEK,
TO FIND,
AND NOT
TO YIELD

ALFRED LORD TENNYSON, 1809–1892

VANITY

Raised by Pemberton
Parentage 'Château de Clos
Vougeot' x seedling
Introduced 1920
Type Hybrid Musk
Size Up to 3m

VEILCHENBLAU

Raised by Schmidt
Parentage 'Crimson Rambler'
x 'Erinnerung an Brod'
Introduced 1909
Type Rambler
Size 5m

VIRIDIFLORA

Raiser and origin Unknown
Introduced Before 1855
Type China
Size 1m

Deep rose-pink, almost single blooms prolifically covering a large plant make 'Vanity' a grand sight. The blooms are at least 10cm across and open out flat and are deliciously fragrant. Perhaps this rose has not achieved the popularity it deserves because of its colour, which some would describe as a rather harsh pink. Nevertheless it is a fine rose and can be made to climb quite easily. Another excellent product from the Pemberton stable.

'Veilchenblau' is a much-talked-about and loved rose that is known all over the world. It has practically no thorns at all and for this reason alone is sought after by some rosarians. But it has much more to offer. It is a gentle but consistent grower and in full bloom is densely covered with small (about 3–4cm), semi-double blooms of several different shades: mauve, lilac, grey, purple and white. The unusual flowers also have a lovely fragrance. This hybrid, along with 'Bleu Magenta', 'Améthyste', 'Rose-Marie Viaud' and 'Violette', form an important group among the Ramblers, all of different shades of purple and mauve.

Another distinctive and different rose that comes from China – a country that holds so many mysteries for westerners. We do not know how long many of the roses in this family were known and appreciated in that country, but we must be forever grateful that they have mostly found their way into our gardens. It could be said that this rose is loved by a few and despised by many. It has greenish, rusty-looking arrangements that serve for flowers and the least you can say is that it is unusual. Roy Rumsey of Dural in New South Wales told me some years ago that several of these flowers suddenly appeared on a red China rose in his garden. Is this the answer to the mystery of where it came from?

WEDDING DAY

Raised by Stern
Parentage R. sinowilsoni
x unknown rose
Introduced 1950
Type Rambler
Size Up to 10m

This is an appropriate name for a rose with white flowers, but it was so named because the flowers first opened on the raiser's wedding anniversary. For twenty years a similar rose has been given this name incorrectly in New Zealand, but the hybrid known in Western Europe as 'Wedding Day' is very different. The genuine one resembles the other but its flowers have a gap between the petals, while the growths and stems are thinner and more wiry. The foliage is a darker green and quite glossy. Until a name can be found for the incorrect one, the original has been called 'English Wedding Day'. Both varieties have smallish white, single, very fragrant blooms in large clusters followed by tiny orange fruit after a summer-long display.

WHITE CÉCILE BRÜNNER

Raised by Fauque
Parentage 'Cécile Brünner' sport
Introduced 1909
Type Polyantha
Size 1m

As this is a colour sport, the shape and composition of the buds and flowers are very similar to the parent, but the foliage is light green and the colour is, of course, quite different. If we became very critical, we could say that this rose is not white but very close to it. The buds are quite yellow in the tight stage, pale to lemon-yellow at first, and then opening to creamy-white later. The flowers are just as freely produced as in the parent and they are also pleasantly fragrant. Even with the number of more modern small roses available this rose is still much sought after for floral work.

WHITE NEW DAWN

Raised by Longley
Parentage 'New Dawn'
x 'Lily Pons'
Introduced 1949
Type Climber
Size 5m

'White New Dawn' is a very valuable addition to the climbers. I saw this rose for the first time in 1988 at the State Rosarium at Sangerhausen in East Germany. Needless to say, I was so impressed with it that it was imported into New Zealand and then released for distribution two years later. It has dark green, healthy foliage with large thorns on the long stems and the young growth is quite dark and bronzy. The flowers are fragrant and medium to large with thirty to thirty-five petals. They are reddish in the bud, opening to a milky-white gardenia-like bloom.

THE SWEETEST
FLOWER
THAT BLOWS

I GIVE YOU AS
WE PART

FOR YOU IT IS
A ROSE

FOR ME IT IS MY
HEART

FREDERICK PETERSON

← *Wedding Day*

WIFE OF BATH

Raised by *David Austin*
Parentage *('Mme Caroline Testout')*
x ('Ma Perkins' x 'Constance Spry')
Introduced *1969*
Type *English Rose*
Size *1.5m*

Tight little buds develop into cupped blooms of clear pink, paling towards the edges. The blooms are medium sized and when open loosely quartered and have a strong fragrance of myrrh. When Seizo Susuki, the noted Japanese rosarian, visited our garden he found the name of this rose amusing and suggested it might be 'Wife in Bath'. Having had some experience of the English language in other countries, I explained that in his country the rose name could have been 'Wife of Tokyo' and that Bath was an English town, not a bathing vessel as he had at first thought. This rose is a tough, compact, repeat-flowering hybrid suitable for small gardens.

← *opposite*

WILLIAM LOBB

Raised by *Laffay*
Parentage *Unknown*
Introduced *1855*
Type *Moss*
Size *2m or more*

'William Lobb' has medium to large flowers with muddled centres, purplish-crimson (more purple than crimson) at first, turning to lavender-purple then greyish lavender with a lighter reverse. The plentiful blooms have a strong scent and look well against the greyish-green foliage. The wood is quite prickly, the buds are well mossed, and the growth, if allowed, can become quite straggly. This rose is sometimes referred to as 'The Old Velvet Rose' and is found in many old gardens and is dear to many hearts. It is a superb old Moss Rose and can be made to climb.

following page ⟶

'TIS THE LAST
ROSE OF SUMMER
LEFT BLOOMING
ALONE;
ALL HER LOVELY
COMPANIONS ARE
FADED AND GONE;
NO FLOWER
OF HER KINDRED,
NO ROSEBUD
IS NIGH,
TO REFLECT BACK
HER BLUSHES,
OR GIVE SIGH
FOR SIGH

← *William Lobb*

THOMAS MOORE, 1779–1852

WILLIAM MORRIS

Raised by David Austin
Parentage 'Abraham Darby'
x unnamed seedling
Introduced 1998
Type English Rose
Size 2m

This beautiful rose is like a larger version of 'Leander', to which it is related. It is extremely hardy and reliable and the flowers are a bright apricot-pink and a nice rosette shape. Strongly fragrant, tall growing and disease resistant, it has glossy foliage and forms a lovely shrub for the back of the border.

←— *opposite*

WINCHESTER CATHEDRAL

Raised by David Austin
Parentage 'Mary Rose' sport
Introduced 1988
Type English Rose
Size 2m

Hybridisers go through the agonising process of painstakingly hand-pollinating parent plants, waiting for the seedpod to ripen, sowing the seed and hoping enough will germinate for a good selection, and then down the track selecting a plant with the required merits. Nature in this case has circumnavigated the process by presenting the hybridiser with a ready-made rose. It is similar to 'Mary Rose' except that it is pure white. It has a lovely scent and the excellent quality of always having some flowers on it.

WINDRUSH

Raised by David Austin
Parentage English Rose seedling
x ('Canterbury' x 'Golden Wings')
Introduced 1984
Type English Rose
Size 2m

Although not really within the confines of the definition of an English Rose, 'Windrush' nevertheless has a double dose of English in it. It resembles 'Golden Wings' in the colour and size of the flowers, which are quite large (13–15cm wide). The buds are yellow and long pointed, grouped five to seven at a time, and the exquisite blooms open wide and semi-double exhibiting golden stamens. The flowers are nicely fragrant. This fine rose could quite easily be made to climb.

WISE PORTIA

Raised by David Austin
Parentage 'The Knight' x
'Glastonbury'
Introduced 1982
Type English Rose
Size 1m

The parents of this excellent rose are the same given for English Rose 'Wenlock', another David Austin rose introduced in 1984. If nothing else, this proves that if someone else were to repeat the process with the same parents it would be practically impossible to achieve the same result. The bush has low, rather spreading growth that is assisted by the large, double, heavy flowers. The blooms come from very fat buds and open wide and well, filled with petals of a genuine old rose character. The colour is at first rich purple, paling a little with age. The blooms have a strong old rose fragrance.

YELLOW BUTTON

Raised by *David Austin*
Parentage *'Wife of Bath' x 'Chinatown'*
Introduced *1975*
Type *English Rose*
Size *1m*

When I first saw this rose in 1985 in England, I thought it was the most beautiful thing I had ever seen. This reaction was quite natural when you remember that up until that time I had spent many years looking at and enjoying the classic old roses and their more restricted colour range. 'Yellow Button' has beautiful blooms of the deepest yolk-yellow in the centre, becoming paler towards the edges. They are rosette-type, quartered and have a button eye, resembling an old rose in every way, but with a modern colour. A strong fruity fragrance pervades the blossoms and the foliage is a light glossy green. Since its introduction, other English Roses such as 'English Garden', 'The Pilgrim', 'Graham Thomas', 'Golden Celebration', 'Molineux', 'Charity', 'Charlotte', 'Happy Child' and 'Buttercup' have joined the yellow section of this wonderful dynasty.

YORK AND LANCASTER

Raiser and origin *Unknown*
Introduced *Before 1629*
Type *Damask*
Size *2m*

Summer flowering only, this fascinating Damask rose has a place in history, not because of any facts about it, but rather its type, its name, and its longevity. The rather leggy growth supports loosely double flowers rather sparingly and the flowers of pink and white and sometimes a little scarlet are quite beautiful and fragrant.

ZÉPHIRINE DROUHIN

Raised by *Bizot*
Parentage *Unknown*
Introduced *1868*
Type *Bourbon climber*
Size *3–4m*

This is a much revered rose that has proved itself since its inception over 130 years ago. The flowers are rich bright pink with a slight trace of cerise in them. The plant is a gentle grower with few thorns and is very well furnished with a massive display of medium to large fragrant blooms, which are double with muddled centres.

WHILE NOT ABLE TO DEVOTE TIME TO HYBRIDISING DURING HIS WORKING
LIFE, TREVOR HAS PRODUCED THIS SMALL GROUP OF ROSE HYBRIDS (WITH THE
EXCEPTION OF FRAU ALBERT HOCHSTRASSER, MENJA AND SIR CEDRIC MORRIS).

| 1 | 2 | 3 |
| 4 | 5 | 6 |

1
ALBATROSS

Raised by *Griffiths*
Parentage *R. moschata x R. multiflora*
Introduced *1988*
Type *Rambler*
Size *5m*

From the parents of this rose one would expect a prolific flowerer, and that is the way this rose performs. It is a rampant grower with long, arching branches covered with medium-sized, sweetly scented, white, single roses in clusters. It is summer-flowering only, and is reminiscent of 'Kiftsgate' at its best, but has prominent golden stamens in the centre.

2
ALICE MAUDE

Raised by *Griffiths*
Parentage *'Roseraie de l'Haÿ' x seedling*
Introduced *1985*
Type *Rugosa Hybrid*
Size *1.5m*

From time to time a rose grower has a variety cross his line of sight and because he has been responsible for the creation he may wish to call it after his mother. This is what happened in this case. The flower of this beautiful variety is the same colour as one of its parents, 'Roseraie de l'Haÿ', but it has a lovely anemone centre with many petals and stamens showing. It is nicely fragrant.

3
ANGELA

Raised by *Griffiths*
Parentage *Seedling x 'Graham Thomas'*
Introduced *1988*
Type *Shrub*
Size *2m*

An exceedingly pretty rose of typical English Rose character, which bears a strong resemblance to 'Graham Thomas'. It has medium to large blooms, which are cupped at first, become quartered, and open out to reflexed flowers of apricot-pink and lemon with a strong fragrance. This rose was named after a young lady who lost her life in a car accident.

4
DARLING DIXIE

Raised by *Griffiths*
Parentage *'Paul's Himalayan Musk' x seedling*
Introduced *1988*
Type *Rambler*
Size *5m*

If you have the need for a vigorous, tough, quick-growing rambler to cover up an old tree, tank stand, farm shed, fence or trellis, then this rose can do all these things, at the same time producing delightful, small (3cm) flowers in clusters, which are the prettiest shade of pale lilac-mauve and are sweetly fragrant. This lovely variety will do the job for you.

5
FRAU ALBERT HOCHSTRASSER

Raised by *Weigand*
Parentage *Unknown*
Introduced *1908*
Type *Rambler*
Size *5m*

Here we have a delightful and vigorous rambler, which I first saw in the State Rosarium in East Germany. It is a lusty grower with healthy foliage and thorny branches, which support a marvellous flowering display of very double medium-sized creamy-white blooms with many petals, a rolled centre, a button eye, and a lovely scent. What more do you want?

6
MENJA

Raised by *Petersen*
Parentage *Unknown*
Introduced *1980*
Type *Hybrid Musk*
Size *1.5m*

This is one of the roses that arrived unexpectedly in a consignment of budwood from Valdemar Petersen of Denmark. This beautiful little rose is different and unusual. The individual blooms are about 3cm wide and appear in large clusters. They are quite deeply cupped and almost single, and of a lovely rich pink at first, fading to blush-pink and white. You could not be blamed for thinking that they were flowers of the shrub Kalmia latifolia.

SIR CEDRIC MORRIS

Raised by *Morris introduced by Peter Beales*
Parentage *R. glauca x seedling*
Introduced *1980*
Type *Climber*
Size *10m or more*

With all our imports from overseas, over many years, from many countries, this would be the strongest and most powerful rose we have ever handled. Jokingly I used to tell people it would grow between the North and South Islands of New Zealand. Of course, with a rose of this type everything is large. The massive branches enveloped a cherry tree 10m high in three seasons. Greyish-green foliage supports a massive display of small, single, white flowers in large clusters over a summer season only.

TREVOR'S FOLLY

Raised by *Griffiths*
Parentage *Unknown*
Introduced *1990*
Type *Rambler*
Size *5m*

This rose appeared as a chance seedling growing up and through a 5m double, white Banksia rose. To have arrived in this position, the seed must have been carried there by the birds. The flowers are single, about 5–6cm across, bright scarlet with a white eye, and appear in nice clusters. If things work out for me, this will be used to create a new race of rambling roses.

CULTIVATION
&
CARE
OF OLD ROSES

As a result of the attitude of some modern gardeners and writers, the cultivation and care of roses has been made to appear too difficult for most people. This misinformation is misguided and possibly stems from the person concerned simply echoing the thoughts of another person, either by word of mouth or by written word, and the advice given is not founded on personal experience.

Having been involved in horticulture in general for more than fifty-five years, and worked with roses in particular for nearly all that time, I can assure the reader that when dealing with nature, one has only to keep things simple to be successful. The soil or ground conditions are the first factors of importance. Roses do not like wet feet and require good drainage. If the site chosen is inclined to hold water, and this does not drain away in a short time, then some sort of drainage or raising of the surface level should be considered.

The next requisite for successful growing is the soil itself. Obviously soil varies greatly over inhabited areas all around the world and, of course, climatic conditions have a big part to play in this. But the basic premise is that it be friable and have moisture retention capability and also draining ability. The actual type of soil does not matter a lot because with the addition of well-chosen materials its texture can be altered. Because rose roots, or for that matter any plant roots, are so sensitive, I would never recommend the addition of manure or fertiliser into the soil where a rose is to be planted. Whatever is required for the future growth of the plant should be placed on the surface, where it can be washed into the soil by hose or rain. Many

people do not realise that plants take up their food supplies by the roots only and therefore during the growing season all food supplies should be applied to the surface of the soil. Many years ago an employer of mine advised me that 'more plants are killed by kindness than ever by neglect'.

Probably the next requirement for good rose culture would be some form of shelter. The nature and composition of a rose plant really demands that it be sheltered, otherwise its foliage and flowers can be decimated in strong winds and rain, and most areas can suffer in this way from time to time. Shelter is not required from all four directions but is needed from at least two. The depth of the planting medium will also have a direct bearing on the growth of the plant.

The treatment of soil is also of great importance. If you are fortunate enough to have a deep, rich, well-drained, loamy soil, you do not need to change very much, but if your soil is sandy or has a heavy clay presence then some changes need to be made. When faced with sandy soils the addition of some type of humus is paramount. Sand on its own will not retain moisture, so some well-rotted material is required, and as this is worked through the sand its particles will retain the necessary moisture to sustain plant life. In the case of clay or volcanic soils, humus will also help to break down the cloggy parts, but the application of lime is perhaps more important because this has the ability to break down the hard parts of clay soil and make it more acceptable to plants. The addition of manures or fertilisers to the surface will always improve the growth of plants, but remember that these applications will promote better weed growth as well.

There has always been debate about the planting of roses, and again this is quite simple. The area above the root system where the graft was placed on the rootstock must be buried below ground level. The very good reason for this is that at that point (about 5cm above the union) there will be three or more branches which will hold the plant steady in the ground against all wind and rain. Rose plants as they grow have more than three-quarters of their volume above the soil level and less than one-quarter below, and this is why those lower branches must be in the soil, where they will eventually root, adding to the overall stability.

Roses do suffer from some pests and diseases, but not nearly as badly as some so-called knowledgeable people would have you believe. The worst pest they seem to suffer from is aphids or green-fly, although depending on the conditions, sometimes attacks come from caterpillars or red mites. However, with the advent of non-poisonous sprays it is not difficult to take charge of the problem and if it is your wish you can resort to some of the older-type sprays still available. There seems to be a great attack of aphids about Labour Weekend (mid-Spring), with lesser ones later in the season.

Three main fungal diseases can affect roses when the conditions suit them. Humidity is the accelerator for these diseases. The best method of treatment for fungal diseases, as well as any insect pests, is to use one of the combined systemic pesticides and fungicides – there are several very good ones available. Many years ago you could purchase separate pesticides and fungicides, which when applied in liquid form had to reach not only the topside of the infected leaves but also the underside, which was nearly impossible to achieve. The modern combined systemics are absorbed right through the leaves, giving a marvellous degree of control. Non-poisonous and organic sprays are now becoming available, and no doubt more advances will be made in this field.

When it comes to the pruning and shaping of roses in all the forms available, again it is not difficult to accomplish, despite what those armchair experts would have you believe. The first thing to remember is that when a plant is cut back, it will invariably send out strong new growth. The harder it is cut, the more it will grow, while the less it is cut, the less it will grow. Roses require trimming to achieve the shape you desire, but where they are trimmed really does not matter. There will always be a need to remove dead wood and unwanted branches, but as long as the whole process remains simple, you will be in harmony with nature.

In summary, the basic requirements for good rose culture are simply as follows:
- Good soil conditions and drainage, either present or created.
- Planting of rose bushes and climbers with the union below ground level.
- Shaping and tidying of plants as and when necessary.
- A limited spraying programme only when necessary.
- Feeding of any kind from the surface only where the particles can be washed into the soil.
- Some measure of shelter.

THE ROSE FAMILY INDEX

DAVID AUSTIN ROSES USED IN THIS BOOK